PRAISE FOR THE BOOK

This is not just a book but a treasure trove of wisdom, offering profound insights for living with purpose, passion and joy. Santosh's abilities to distil the complexities of life in 50 simple yet powerful rules is commendable and I am deeply impressed with the clarity and depth with which he has articulated each concept. I wish Santosh all the success and fulfilment that he so generously encourage others to seek. May his words continue to inspire, uplift and transform lives.

Nitin Gadkari
Minister, Road Transport and Highways, Govt. of India

May this book be a light on your journey, helping you to rediscover the joy, peace, and purpose that are your birth right. As you read and reflect, may these teachings not only touch your mind but also open your heart, awakening the divine flow within you and enriching your life beyond measure.

Swami Chidanand Saraswati
President, Parmarth Niketan, Rishikesh

In today's volatile, uncertain, complex, and ambiguous (VUCA) world where attention spans are getting shorter and time is becoming scarce, this book of 50 practical and easy-to-adopt life Sutras is a must-have navigation tool to meet challenges successfully.

GP Hinduja
Chairman, Hinduja Group

In an age of cut throat competition, leading to greater stress levels, the 50 rules laid down in this book act as a lighthouse especially for the youth of today to navigate these turbulent and disruptive times. Thank you for bringing this book to life.

Rajesh Parmeswaran
Executive Director and Industrial Sector Leader, IBM India

This book 50 Golden Rules of Life, felt like a compassionate friend, holding my hand & guiding me in every situation. It reminded me of my own strength, helping me rediscover my resilience. It gently whispers to you, that you are never truly alone, even in your toughest times.

Ambreen Zaidi
Award-winning Journalist, Author and Columnist

I am happy that you wrote the book in the format that you did. I think after reading the examples in your book, it will be beneficial for anyone to keep a screenshot of your table of contents page close by for easy access to remind them of the 50 Golden Rules of Life to live a happy and fulfilling life.

Veera Mahajan
Mediator, Life Coach, TEDx Speaker, Best-Selling Author, and Producer

---

50 Golden Rules of Life encourages you to embark on a journey of self-improvement and fulfilment, providing practical insights to live with purpose and joy. Keep it close, and let it inspire and uplift you, one golden rule at a time.

Dr Tripta Thakur
Director General, National Power Training Institute, Ministry of Power, Govt. of India

---

Discover fifty essential principles for a fulfilling life in 50 Golden Rules of Life by Santosh Joshi, a book that inspires growth and meaningful existence.

Sanjay Dubey
IAS, Additional Chief Secretary, IT, Science and Technology and GAD, Govt. of MP

An outstanding book! What Santosh, as an author brings out in the book, is something very relevant in today's times. A must-read for anyone who wishes to take a quantum jump in their life in terms of joy, fulfilment, and success.

Brajesh Kumar Upadhyay
Chairman & Managing Director, Goa Shipyard Ltd, Dept. of Defence Production, Ministry of Defence, Govt. of India

---

Whether you are seeking clarity, motivation, or a fresh perspective, this book provides the tools and insights to help you navigate your journey with confidence and grace. Embrace these rules, and transform the ordinary into the extraordinary.

Sunil Kharbanda
Co-Founder & CRO, TreZix Software Private Limited

---

50 GOLDEN RULES OF LIFE

TIMELESS STRATEGIES FOR SUCCESS, FULFILMENT, AND INNER PEACE

SANTOSH JOSHI

50 GOLDEN RULES OF LIFE

TIMELESS STRATEGIES FOR SUCCESS, FULFILMENT, AND INNER PEACE

SANTOSH JOSHI

EMBASSY BOOKS
www.embassybooks.in

First Edition 2024
Published in India by:
Embassy Book Distributors
120, Great Western Building, Maharashtra Chamber of
Commerce Lane, Fort, Mumbai 400 023, India
Tel: (+9122) -30967415, 22819546
Email: info@embassybooks.in
www.embassybooks.in

ISBN: 978-81-19726-79-0

Distribution Centres:
Mumbai, Ahmedabad, Bangalore, Kolkata, Chennai, Hyderabad,
New Delhi, Pune

Cover Design by Sonal Churi

Layout and typesetting by Sonal Churi &
Gangaram Dhuri (Brand Soul Creations)

Printed & bound in India by Parksons Graphics Pvt. Ltd.

TABLE OF CONTENTS

| PREFACE

From a young age, I was captivated by the stories of sages who meditated in the Himalayas or under banyan trees, or ascetics enduring harsh weather in search of truth. I dreamt of one day travelling to the Himalayas, meditating, and achieving nirvana.

However, as I grew older, life took its own course. My career flourished, I got married, changed jobs, and my ageing parents needed my time and attention. These events unfolded so rapidly that my dream of going to the Himalayas seemed ever more distant.

Yet, through life's ups and downs, I realised that the answers and truths I sought were within the very life I was living. You do not need to go to the Himalayas to find what you are looking for. With each difficulty and challenge you face in life you climb one mountain. Some peaks are easy to climb while some are treacherous. But if you are able to surmount those, the feeling is no less than nirvana. These hills of everyday challenges offer invaluable lessons at every step, helping us evolve and grow. Though life is chaotic, there is peace hidden within the chaos, waiting to be discovered.

Many believe that only asceticism and renunciation can lead one to wisdom. However, my experiences have shown me that distancing oneself from life's experiences actually takes one away from true wisdom. Wisdom is gained by facing and overcoming challenges, each one revealing hidden insights. This process continues throughout our lives, allowing us to accumulate wisdom. It is akin to an old video game where you collect gold coins after each level, advancing to higher stages.

Each of us is on a unique journey, and life presents us with tailor-made lessons necessary for our growth. For instance, I learnt an important lesson from caring for my mother, who had Alzheimer's. Initially, her repetitive actions irritated me, but over time, they taught me one of the greatest virtues – patience. I also learnt empathy as I began to understand her condition. This period allowed me to shower her with unconditional love, even when she could not recognise me. These experiences, among other challenges, humbled me.

Life offers ample opportunities to learn and evolve. We learn from the people around us, our relationships, our reactions to situations, how we handle our emotions, discovering our purpose, what brings us joy, and how we can help others. We just need to be good students – curious, open-minded, accepting, and eager to learn.

Life is an intricate tapestry woven with moments of joy, sorrow, triumphs, and challenges. Navigating through its complexities can sometimes feel overwhelming, leaving us in search of guidance and wisdom to lead a fulfilling and meaningful life. *50 Golden Rules of Life* is a collection of timeless principles designed to offer that guidance, providing a roadmap to live with purpose, passion and joy.

Over the years, I have been fortunate to gather profound wisdom from my experiences, interactions, and reflections. This book is born out of a deep desire to share that wisdom with you. Life's journey is enriched when we can learn from each other, and through this book, I aim to give back to society some of the insights that have significantly shaped my own path.

This book is structured to be both a reflective companion and a practical guide. Each chapter delves into a vital aspect of life, offering insights with examples and stories, reflections, and actionable advice. Whether you are seeking to enhance your personal wellbeing, build stronger relationships, or find deeper meaning in your daily experiences, these golden rules serve as beacons to illuminate your path. You could keep it on your bedside table as a handy pick-me-up, and turn open any chapter whenever you seek inspiration or hope – often, the page you land on would have just the words you need to read that day.

The chapters are thoughtfully arranged to cover various dimensions of life. From starting your day with a positive thought to regularly connecting with your inner self, each rule is a piece of the puzzle that, when put together, creates a holistic approach to living a fulfilling and purposeful life.

Santosh Joshi

#1 | START YOUR DAY WITH A POSITIVE THOUGHT

Lilian Wu was a meticulous and highly regarded pastry chef at a famous bakery in Wan Chai, Hong Kong. She was known for her creativity and precision. One morning, as Lilian was preparing to leave for work, she accidentally knocked over a precious vase that had belonged to her grandmother. The crash echoed through her small apartment, and she felt a wave of sadness.

"Great, just great," she mumbled to herself. "Today is already ruined."

Carrying this negative thought with her, Lilian Wu left for work in a sullen mood. As she rode the metro, she could not shake off the image of the broken vase. By the time she arrived at the bakery, she was distracted and irritable.

In the kitchen, her negative mindset began to manifest in small, but impactful ways. She misread a recipe, resulting in a dough that was too dry. When a colleague asked for her opinion on a new cake, she snapped at him. Throughout the day, she made several uncharacteristic mistakes. Her sour mood even affected customer interactions. Regular customers, who were used to her warm and friendly nature, noticed her curt responses and distant attitude.

As the day drew to a close, Lilian Wu realised how one negative thought had spiralled out of control, casting a shadow over her entire day. Reflecting on the events, she understood the power of her mindset and how crucial it was to address negative thoughts before they could take root and spread.

In ancient Japan, samurai warriors would begin their day with a ritual known as *Kanzen*.

Kanzen embodies a holistic approach that balances mind, body, and spirit. Rooted in centuries-old traditions, it typically begins with a mindful morning ritual of stretching to awaken the body gently. This is followed by a brief practice of meditative reflection, allowing for mental clarity and focus. This includes setting clear intentions or goals, and creating a sense of purpose and direction for the day ahead. The ritual ends with a nutritious, well-balanced breakfast featuring seasonal ingredients to provide the necessary energy for the day ahead. By integrating these elements, this ancient practice emphasises the power of a positive and harmonious start to the day, encouraging a mindful and productive mindset that aligns with the principles of balance and intentional living.

Your mind is not only your most trusted friend but also your biggest enemy. A small negative thought has the capacity to give rise to a chain of negative thoughts affecting your entire day. The reverse is also true. A small positive thought can give rise to a positive chain of thoughts creating a purposeful and positive day.

Our thoughts determine our actions, behaviour, and our attitude. Like seeds, our thoughts can sprout and grow big depending on the fertilisers and nurturance we give them in terms of energy and attention. Humankind's greatest discoveries and biggest acts of destruction have sprung from a single thought.

The first thoughts in the morning set the tone for the day. Hence, it is of utmost importance that you start your day with a positive thought.

Sometimes, even if you wake up with a bad dream, after a disturbed sleep, or with physical pain, or something goes wrong in the morning, understand that your thoughts have the power to influence your state of mind. By consciously choosing a positive thought, you can shift your focus and set a positive tone for the day ahead. It uplifts your mood, boosts your energy, and enhances your overall wellbeing. It sets the stage for a day filled with gratitude and optimism.

So, tomorrow morning when you wake up, make a conscious effort to choose a positive thought. Nurture it, let it grow, and witness how it transforms your entire day. Embrace the power of your thoughts and tap into the limitless potential they hold.

Things you can do for a positive start to your day:

- Smile at yourself when you look at the mirror while brushing your teeth.
- Thank the universe for a good night's sleep and everything you have.
- Say these affirmations loudly every morning, with full conviction and belief:
  - — Today is the happiest day of my life
  - — Today is the day of that turning point I was waiting for
  - — I feel healthy, strong, and powerful today
  - — I have all that I need to make today a great day

Golden Rule:

A single positive thought in the morning can set the tone for a day of gratitude, optimism, and courage.

#2 ALWAYS ANCHOR IN YOUR CORE VALUES

Jonathan was sailing a boat across a vast ocean. He was the captain, guiding his vessel towards land. The boat had somehow lost its compass, and hence he had to use the North Star for direction. Everything was going well until, suddenly, a storm rolled in, hiding the North Star behind dark clouds. Waves and harsh rain lashed at the sides of the boat. The deck was soaked, and so was Jonathan. Loud thunder and lightning made the scene scarier.

As the strong winds and huge waves tossed his boat, he began to feel lost without a sense of direction. He was also worried that his boat may overturn and sink due to the power of wind and waves. What would a good captain do in this situation?

Assessing the strength of the storm and the depth of the sea, Jonathan decided to drop anchor. The anchor dug into the seabed, keeping the boat steady until the storm passed. When the storm finally calmed down, the dark clouds disappeared, and he could see the North Star again.

With the storm gone and the North Star shining bright, Jonathan pulled up the anchor and continued sailing towards his destination.

In this anecdote, the boat is a metaphor for your life, the land represents your life goal, and the North Star is your motivation. When the storms of life make you feel lost, you lose sight of your motivation. Your life is tossed around by the waves of adversities and winds of challenges. In such situations, the best way to steady yourself is to anchor yourself to your core values, until you find your way again.

The core values we inherently possess as humans are like precious gems bestowed upon us at birth. Love, compassion, empathy, sensitivity, kindness, gratitude, faith, forgiveness, courage, honesty, truthfulness, trust, hope, humility, peace, patience, and acceptance reside deep within us, waiting to be nurtured and embraced.

An interesting point to note here is that you do not need to anchor yourself to all core values simultaneously. Instead, choose one or two that resonate most with you, or which you feel are closest to your heart. By anchoring yourself to these, you will find that other core values will naturally fall into place.

For instance, in challenging times, if you anchor yourself to faith, you will find that patience, hope, courage, and acceptance will follow suit. Similarly, if you anchor yourself to gratitude and appreciate everything you are blessed with, core values of humility, faith, compassion, sensitivity, kindness, forgiveness, and acceptance will naturally become part of you too.

Although one cannot do complete justice to define each core value in just a few lines as these are much deeper and more complex subjects, let us examine them briefly:

Love: An emotion that is deeper than just profound affection and care for others. At its core, love involves selflessness, empathy, and a genuine desire for the wellbeing of others.

Compassion: The heartfelt desire to ease the suffering of others, often leading to acts of kindness and support, encouraging a sense of community and interconnectedness.

Empathy: The ability to understand and share another person's feelings, creating a meaningful connection and promoting mutual understanding and compassion.

Sensitivity: Awareness and consideration of the emotions and feelings of others, which helps in avoiding hurt and nurturing harmonious and respectful interactions.

Kindness: The quality of being generous, considerate, and friendly towards others. It involves showing care, compassion, and a willingness to help without expecting anything in return.

Gratitude: The feeling of thankfulness and appreciation for the good things in life, whether they are tangible or intangible. It involves recognising and acknowledging the kindness of others, the beauty of everyday moments, and the positive aspects of one's experiences.

Faith: A strong belief or trust in something, often without requiring evidence, logic, or condition. It can either be seen as confidence in the universe and its process, or trust in the dependability and goodness of people and outcomes. It can also mean belief in self or trust in one's own capabilities. Faith gives rise to hope, strength, and resilience, helping one to navigate challenges and uncertainties of life with a sense of purpose and assurance.

Forgiveness: The conscious decision to release feelings of resentment and anger toward someone who has harmed you. It includes letting go of negative emotions and thoughts related to the wrongdoing, allowing for emotional healing and personal peace.

Courage: The strength to face fear, pain, danger, uncertainty, or adversity. It involves taking bold actions or making difficult decisions despite potential risks or challenges. It allows one to follow one's goals with determination and resilience.

Honesty: The quality of being straightforward, sincere, and free from deceit. It involves being transparent in one's actions and intentions, and upholding integrity at all times.

Truthfulness: The habit of saying what is right. It highlights the importance of being genuine and reliable in both speech and behaviour.

Trust: The firm belief in the reliability and integrity of someone or something. It means one has the confidence that others will act in a fair, honest, and dependable manner. It forms the foundation for a secure and stable relationship.

Hope: The feeling of expectation for a positive outcome or future. It means optimism and a belief that good things will happen, even in the face of challenges or uncertainty. Hope gives motivation and takes one through difficult times, bringing out determination and resilience.

Humility: The virtue of having a modest view of one's own importance. It means recognising and accepting one's limitations, being open to learning from others, and valuing their contributions.

Peace: A state of calmness and harmony, characterised by the presence of contentment and absence of conflict, anxiety, or agitation. It mainly refers to inner stillness and tranquillity.

Patience: The ability to go through delay, difficulty, or disturbance without becoming angry or upset. It means maintaining composure and calmly waiting for the desired outcome.

Acceptance: When one embraces situations, circumstances, or people as they are, without trying to change or resist them. It happens when one acknowledges the reality with openness and without judgement, allowing for inner peace.

As we journey through life, we encounter various experiences that shape our beliefs and perspectives. Society's influence often veers us away from our core values, tempting us to take shortcuts and compromising our moral compass. In the pursuit of worldly success and gain, we may unintentionally stray from the virtues that once guided us.

Yet, when the storms of life shake the very foundations of our existence, we must seek solace in our core values. Just as a ship steadies itself by dropping anchor, we too can find stability and strength by reconnecting with the principles that define us.

Embracing our core values becomes our compass, guiding us through the darkest of storms and leading us back to calmer waters. They serve as unwavering beacons, illuminating the path towards a meaningful and purposeful life. No matter the challenges we face or the obstacles that obstruct our way, adhering to our core values ensures that we remain true to ourselves and our innate goodness.

When we consistently anchor ourselves in these values, our journey through life becomes smoother. We become resilient, unperturbed by the trials and tribulations that come our way. Our resolve becomes unshakeable, and we are not swayed by unfavourable circumstances or the actions of others.

We find strength in our integrity, comfort in our empathy, and serenity in our peace. These values become the armour that shields us from negativity, providing a solid foundation upon which we can rebuild when life knocks us down.

Golden Rule:

***When life's storms arise,
anchor yourself in your core values
to find stability and direction.***

#3 | LOOK AT THE WORLD AS A MIRROR

A person asked a wise man, "Why is everybody in this world so selfish? Why are people not true to each other?"

The wise man smiled and told him a story.

Once, in a small village, there was a room filled with mirrors. A little girl used to go inside and play there every day. Seeing hundreds of children around her in the mirrors made her joyful. She would clap her hands and all the children would clap back at her.

She considered this place the world's most beautiful place and would be very happy being there.

One other time, a sad and angry person visited this room filled with mirrors. What he saw around him were hundreds of angry men staring at him. He got scared and raised his hands to hit them and in return all hands lifted to hit him back.

He thought this was the worst place in the world and left it.

"So," the wise man said, "this world is also a room filled with mirrors around you. We see our own image in the mirrors. What we give to the universe is what the universe will give back to us."

The world operates much like a mirror, reflecting back the actions and attitudes we project into it. When we approach life with positivity, kindness, and understanding, we often find these same qualities mirrored back to us in our interactions and experiences. On the other hand, if we operate out of negativity, anger, and resentment, the world tends to respond in kind, creating a cycle of adverse outcomes. The world mirrors our own actions and attitudes, responding to what we emanate.

Our perception about us shapes our reality as well. The lens through which we view ourselves ultimately colours the world we see. Just as a distorted mirror will reflect a distorted image, if we see ourselves through a lens of kindness, compassion, empathy, love, humility, and trust, we will encounter these very virtues in those who surround us. This reflective nature of the world highlights the importance of cultivating a positive mindset and compassionate behaviour, as these not only shape our own reality but also influence the broader environment around us.

Our interactions with others are particularly telling examples of this mirror effect. If we constantly find faults and mistakes in others, treating them with mistrust and a sense of superiority, we inadvertently invite similar behaviour towards us. A smile can cause a smile in return, while an unkind word can incite defensiveness or hostility. By consciously choosing to act with empathy and integrity, we set off a chain reaction of goodwill that can significantly enhance our relationships and overall quality of life.

This reflective principle encourages self-awareness and personal responsibility, reminding us that we have the power to shape our world through our own attitudes and actions. In essence, the world is a reflection of who we are, and by striving to be our best selves, we create a more positive and harmonious reality.

Golden Rule:

The world reflects our attitudes and actions, giving back what we project.

#4 LOVE YOURSELF UNCONDITIONALLY

Margaret was of medium height with a rosy complexion and warm, expressive eyes. Living in a small apartment with her mother, her life seemed simple and uneventful and her behaviour gentle and modest. However, there was a quiet strength about her, suggesting a deep inner world and unspoken dreams. Margaret was kind-hearted and would not leave any opportunity to help somebody. But when it came to herself, she was her own harshest critic. She worked at a clerical position in a large company and often felt overlooked and invisible. She would frequently tell herself, "You are worthless. See, no one even acknowledges your existence." And so, Margaret spent her life hidden in a shell she created around herself.

One morning, on her way to work, Margaret spotted a new hat shop down the street. Curious, she decided to step inside and check out the hats. After trying out a few, she found one that looked really beautiful. The first to notice was a little girl there who said, "Mommy, look how pretty that woman looks with the hat on." Margaret was taken aback, as nobody had complimented her in a long time. A second buyer also commented, "Ma'am, you look lovely with that hat on." Margaret again looked at herself in the mirror and this time something magical happened – something changed. For the first time, she saw herself differently; she felt love towards the person in the mirror.

She decided to buy the hat. Feeling a new sense of excitement, she went to the counter and made the payment. As she stepped outside, the world seemed to come alive with vibrant colours and music that she had never noticed before. Margaret walked with a spring in her step, feeling as though she were floating on clouds.

Arriving at the office building, the doorman greeted her with a warm, "Good morning," a gesture that had never happened before. Inside the office, her colleagues showered her with compliments, as if seeing her in a new light. Even her boss took notice of her. Throughout the day, Margaret basked in the glow of her newfound confidence, experiencing a sense of joy and appreciation she had never known.

Treating herself to a cab ride home, Margaret reflected on the miraculous day she had had, attributing it all to the power of her new hat. When she got home, her mom opened the door. The sight of Margaret took her breath away. "Margaret," she said, surprised. "How beautiful you look!"

"Yes, mother," said Margaret. "It's all thanks to my new hat. I had the most marvellous day." Her mother looked at her again and asked, "What hat?" Margaret panicked. She touched her head and realised that the hat that had changed her life was not there. She did not remember taking it off in the cab, or at the office. She thought back to the store where she had bought it. Then she remembered, painfully, that she had forgotten the hat right there, on the counter. And she had walked out to the street – hatless, yet glowing.

That day, Margaret learnt that true beauty did not come from the 'hat' but it came from within. Acknowledging the unconditional love she felt for herself changed everything around her.

We live in a world of comparison and perfectionism. We often let society decide who we are and believe in the identity that society gives us based on our goals, successes, network, and financial status. Nothing we do is 'ever enough' for society, which leads us to see our own flaws and to criticise ourselves. We often compare ourselves to others and sabotage our self-worth.

But in reality, each one of us is a unique person with unique experiences, thought processes, looks, talents, and characteristics that set us apart from the rest of the world – and that is our identity. That is what we truly are and that is what we need to cherish by loving ourselves unconditionally. We need to stop comparing ourselves with others and to start celebrating our individuality. This will unlock the power of self-love.

For cultivating self-love, it is important to take care of

self – physically, mentally, and emotionally. Set aside some dedicated time for yourself, do some physical activity that makes you feel good about your body, pamper yourself with a massage, and dress smartly. Regular introspection and awareness of your thoughts and emotions are also essential. Engage in activities that bring you joy and ignite your passion. Replace self-doubt with affirmations of self-worth such as,

I love, accept, and approve of myself as I am

I am the best

I am successful in whatever I do

I deserve all good things in life

I am beautiful and lovable

I am complete in all respects

Make yourself a priority in your life. Establish boundaries, learn to say 'no' to what does not serve you, and prioritise your wellbeing. It will slowly and steadily bring a shift in the way you think about yourself and you will start loving the person that you are.

There is another powerful exercise in cultivating self-love. Take a hand mirror and look into it. Initially what you see is a reflection of yourself. Go beyond that reflection and dive deep. You will meet a completely different person than you had imagined – lovable, strong, creative, empathetic, kind and beautiful – a person you will fall in love with. Acknowledge and promise to love that 'you,' unconditionally. While doing this exercise keep your inner critic at bay. This exercise has a cathartic effect and you are sure to experience a shift within.

By practising self-love, you become your own best friend who is non-judgemental and always by your side. You attract positivity, cultivate inner peace and a profound sense of contentment that radiates through all aspects of your life. Remember, you are deserving of the same kindness and acceptance you freely offer to others.

Golden Rule:

Embrace your flaws, celebrate your strengths, and cherish the beautiful person you are, because true happiness and fulfilment stem from loving yourself unconditionally.

#5 | BELIEVE IN MIRACLES

Miracles are moments that defy logic and science, evoking awe and wonder. They change lives, give hope in tough times, and show us the amazing power of belief. Throughout history, stories of miracles have inspired us, proving there is a magical side to life that we cannot always explain.

Miracles often appear in the most unexpected places and times, offering a glimmer of hope in the darkest of moments.

After the devastating earthquake in Haiti in 2010, rescuers found a four-month-old baby named Landina Seignon alive after being buried under rubble for four days. Landina was so dehydrated that her veins had collapsed and the doctor had to put a needle through her shinbone and directly into her bone marrow to deliver fluids. Despite it all, she survived. Her survival against such overwhelming odds was considered a miracle and brought hope to many in the disaster's aftermath. Landina was famously known as the miracle baby of Haiti. In times of crisis, stories like this serve as powerful reminders that miracles can and do happen, even in the most unlikely circumstances.

Miracles can be found in everyday life, often in subtle and unexpected ways. A miracle can be a sudden recovery from illness, a serendipitous encounter that changes the course of one's life, or a moment of profound insight that brings clarity and peace.

Recently, a relative of mine was in a terrible accident, resulting in a fractured hip bone that required immediate surgery. Rushed to the nearest hospital, the doctors performed a successful operation. However, just as they were finishing, he suffered a major heart stroke and was placed on life support. The doctors, seeing no hope, informed the family to prepare for the worst.

When the gut-wrenching decision was made to turn off the ventilator, the son asked to see his father one last time. Sitting beside him, holding his hand, the son, with tears streaming down his face, whispered, "I will miss you, Dad." At that very moment, he felt a slight squeeze and looked up, only to see his father's eyes slowly opening, gazing back at him. Incredibly, against all odds, his father had come back to life just as he was about to be declared dead. This was nothing less than a miracle.

Science, too, has its share of miracles. Medical advancements that once seemed impossible are now routine. Organ transplants, life-saving medications, and groundbreaking treatments for diseases are modern miracles that save lives daily.

Nature itself is a testimony of miracles. Every sunrise, the changing seasons, the birth of a new life, rustling of leaves in the wind, vibrant colours of a sunset, and the resilience of ecosystems are everyday miracles that often go unnoticed. As a matter of fact, every moment is a miracle. Every breath we take, the food we ingest, the pumping of our heart, the way our body works, is a miracle.

Miracles often occur when we least expect them, challenging our understanding of what is possible and reminding us of the mysteries of life. They inspire us to look beyond the surface, to see the beauty in the ordinary, and to hold onto hope even in the face of adversity.

To experience a miracle, one needs to open one's heart to see the unseen, hear the unheard, and experience the unexperienced. **When you look at the world with wonder in your eyes, you start to see the extraordinary in the ordinary.** Each day becomes an opportunity to discover something new, to appreciate the small miracles that surround us, and to feel a deep connection to the world. This perspective transforms everyday experiences into magical moments, enriching our lives with a sense of gratitude and wonder.

George was the only person left alive on a small island after a plane crash. He cried and prayed to the universe asking for help. This went on for a few days but nobody came to rescue him. Tired of waiting, he made a shelter to protect himself and his few possessions.

One day, he went hunting for food, and lightning struck the island. On his return, he found his shelter on fire. Everything he had owned after the crash was gone in big bursts of smoke. He was furious and said to the universe, "I asked for your help. Why did you do this to me?" Heartbroken, he fell asleep on the sand.

Next morning, he woke up to the sound of a boat close to the island. They were rescuers from a ship passing by. He asked them how they knew he was there. The rescuers said that they had seen the smoke signals he made the previous day.

Like George, we often get mad and lose faith in the universe because things do not happen as we wish them to. If we look at those things in retrospect, we will realise that everything happens for a reason – that a miracle was in the making.

If we join the dots in our life, we will find a pattern. This is commonly known as synchronicity. Synchronicity is occurrence of meaningful coincidences that seem to have no cause. We just need to understand that we are all part of a larger plan, and are slowly being guided to what we are here for. Each experience, incident, or a person we come across in life is there because they guide us towards a direction. The incidents that we perceive as negative or unfavourable have, in fact, some deep hidden lessons in them and are for our larger good. We need to just play our part in this drama called life and believe unconditionally in the universal process. And when we practise this, we will witness miracles happening at every step.

When we change our perspective of looking at life, we will see that our life itself is a miracle. And when we see every moment with wonderment, our journey becomes beautiful and filled with meaning.

Everything in the universe, from the tiniest atoms to the vast galaxies, is in a constant state of flux and vibration. Modern science has provided ample proof of this theory over the years. It also says that each entity vibrates at a unique frequency, which is why everything appears distinct from one another. We humans keep changing the frequency of our vibrations from the time of our birth till our final moment.

When we are born, we arrive into this world vibrating at a higher frequency. At this frequency, we are inherently connected to the purpose of our life. We possess boundless potential and have access to universal wisdom. We are aware of our mission of life and the path we need to traverse. However, as we grow older, our vibrations begin to diminish. The societal conditioning and the belief patterns we adopt gradually lower our frequency. We become enveloped in layers that distance us from our true selves.

In this process, we forget that we are here for a reason. We forget about the immense potential and wisdom we possess to reach our goals. As our frequency decreases, we start perceiving life as a continuous struggle, and we convince ourselves that we cannot manifest our best life. We stop believing in miracles and accept that life is a misery. Consequently, we live our lives externally, constantly entwined with the lower frequencies of the world around us until we begin to resonate with them. An interesting fact here is that we attract whatever we resonate with, including people. **Our vibe attracts our tribe.**

Fortunately, it is possible to raise our vibrations and re-establish our connection to the frequency we were vibrating at, at the time of birth. By assessing the quality of our thoughts and what we prioritise in life, we can gauge our current frequency. To elevate our vibrations, we can employ various practical methods such as self-introspection, meditation and relaxation, spending time in nature, engaging in creative pursuits or engaging in physical activities or therapies.

As we resonate with our higher frequency, we begin to manifest our thoughts and desires. Life transforms into a canvas where we can paint our dreams into reality. Miracles become a part of life rather than by chance. By raising our vibrations, we not only reconnect with our purpose, potential, and wisdom but also unlock the ability to manifest the best possible life for ourselves.

Golden Rule:

Cherish the miracles in everyday life, for they remind us of the extraordinary power of belief and the hidden magic that shapes our existence.

#6 | KNOW YOUR PRIORITIES

A philosophy professor carried out an interesting experiment. He brought two similar glass jars, a box of sand, pebbles, and some rocks.

The professor stood before his eager students, holding the first empty jar. Placing it in front of him, he filled it with sand and pebbles and then tried to put the rocks. But the jar was already full, so it could not accommodate the rocks.

Looking at this the students were a little confused. The professor then took the second jar. And this time, he reversed the process. He first put the rocks, then the pebbles and then the sand. Everything fitted in except some sand.

Leaning in, the professor shared the wisdom behind the exercise. "This jar represents your life," he began, gesturing toward the now-filled container. "The rocks symbolise the most important facets of your existence – family, health, relationships, self-growth. Even if all else is lost, these remain, giving your life purpose and meaning."

Gesturing to the pebbles, he continued, "The pebbles represent the secondary elements of your life – work, education, finances. While significant, they are not essential to your overall wellbeing and may come and go."

Finally, indicating the sand, he explained, "The sand signifies the small and insignificant things and material possessions that fill your days but hold little significance in the grand scheme of things."

Pausing for effect, he delivered the moral of the story. "If you fill your life with sand – trivialities and distractions – you leave little room for the rocks, the truly important things in life. Prioritise the rocks in your life, and the pebbles and sand will naturally find their place around them."

The students received a valuable lesson of life and a newfound understanding – to live a purposeful life, one must first prioritise what truly matters, leaving space for the essential while tending to the rest in due time.

We have limited time, energy, and resources while on this planet. And we need to use them judiciously. While doing all the stuff that is of least importance – which is the 'sand' in the above experiment – we are using up the resources available to us. These things could be spending excessive time on social media, shopping, gossiping, worrying, comparing, arguing, and so on. These are the things that distract us from moving ahead in life. Later in life, it dawns upon us that we could not do what we wanted to, leading to regrets.

Prioritising things in life is of utmost importance as this becomes the guiding principle that shapes our actions, decisions, and ultimately our lives. This represents what matters most to us, reflecting our values, aspirations, and long-term goals. Just as a sculptor chisels away at a block of marble to reveal the masterpiece within, setting priorities allows us to carve out a life of purpose and significance from the chaos of daily existence.

Golden Rule:

Prioritise the essential aspects of your life to ensure a meaningful and balanced existence.

#7 | AVOID PROCRASTINATION

In a small village, there lived a young man named Leo who was infamous for his procrastination. Leo had big dreams and many talents, but he always found an excuse to delay his tasks. One day, while wandering, he stumbled upon an old, unusual shop filled with strange gadgets and artifacts.

Leo entered the shop with curiosity. Among the various items, a peculiar clock caught Leo's eye. The clock had an inscription that read, 'The Procrastination Clock: Time Waits for No One.' The elderly shopkeeper explained that the clock had the magical power to show the future consequences of procrastination. Intrigued, Leo bought the clock and took it home.

That night, as he pondered over his unfinished projects, he set the clock to a future date when he had planned to achieve his goals. To his amazement, the clock projected a hologram of his future self – tired, frustrated, and filled with regret over missed opportunities. Shaken by the vision, Leo realised the impact of his procrastination. Determined to change, he began to use the clock as a motivational tool. Each time he felt the urge to delay a task, he would set the clock to a future date and see the potential negative result. The vivid images of a life filled with regret and missed opportunities spurred him into action.

Leo began to complete tasks on time and to pursue his passions. His newfound efficiency brought him success and fulfilment. Word of Leo's remarkable change spread through the village, and he became a respected mentor, helping others to realise the importance of acting on time and not putting off their dreams. He credited his transformation to the mysterious Procrastination Clock, which had shown him the stark reality of a life wasted in procrastination.

Here is an interesting way to understand this.

At present, the average life expectancy of humans globally is a little over 70 years (some of us may be luckier to be alive and kicking till 100 or more). That's 70 years to do what we wish to do in life. Suppose you are 35 years old. You have 35 more years to achieve your goals. When you multiply 35 by 365, you get 12,775 days. Practically speaking, that is all you have to accomplish what you wish to in your life.

Most often, we take life for granted. When we say, "Oh, I will do it next day or next week or next year," we are losing those many days from our cache. So, we need to look at life from this perspective; only then will we appreciate the urgency.

Procrastination happens when we keep pushing things off,

thinking we will do them later. But the problem is, later can turn into never. Sometimes, it is because we are scared to fail or because we want everything to be perfect. Other times, we just do not feel like doing it. Whatever the reason, procrastination stops us from reaching our goals.

Have you ever noticed that the longer you wait to do something, the less likely you are to actually do it? This is known as the Law of Diminishing Intent, and it can be a major roadblock to achieving your goals.

When we first decide to do something, we are full of enthusiasm and motivation. However, as time goes by, our enthusiasm starts to wane and other things can take priority. The longer we put things off, the harder it becomes to actually follow through.

To overcome the law of diminishing intent, it is important to take action as soon as possible after making a decision. Start initiating steps today, and watch as your momentum builds and you make progress towards your goals.

How do we stop procrastinating and start getting things done?

Set clear goals: Figure out what you want to achieve and make a plan of action. This makes it easier to stick to your vision.

Take small steps: Big tasks can be overwhelming. Break them into smaller, more manageable chunks, and tackle them one at a time.

Set deadlines: Give yourself deadlines to finish tasks. It helps to keep you focused and motivated.

Cut out distractions: Identify what distracts you and try to minimise those distractions. It could be your phone, social media, or even noisy surroundings.

Be kind to yourself: It is okay to slip up sometimes. Instead of beating yourself up about it, try to learn from it and keep moving forward.

Time is precious, and every day counts. By understanding 'why' we procrastinate, and taking steps to overcome it, we can make the most of the time we have.

Golden Rule:

Stop putting things off and start making things happen.

#8 | EMBRACE FAILURES

I was at the pinnacle of my career when I left my cushy corporate job of 17 years and chose to follow my purpose. I became a Life Coach and Regression Therapist. Although I had faith in the universe and confidence in my abilities, I was clueless about what life was going to throw at me. I did not know that, in the very beginning of my new journey, I would be walking a rugged trail. I had to face numerous challenges and setbacks. Nothing was easy. Every time I failed, I felt miserable, as if the whole universe was conspiring against me. Often, I felt like giving up and returning to my comfort zone – my corporate job.

Despite the tough times, every time I felt like quitting, I found something to hold on to that kept me moving forward. I realised that every failure taught me something valuable and amazing. It reminded me of what Thomas Edison once said: "I have not failed. I've just found 10,000 ways that won't work."

Viewing failure in this new light made it interesting. I started to think creatively and invent new approaches. Each setback became a stepping stone that led me to where I am today. It became clear to me that the universe was actually working in my favour.

I soon found out that success and failure are subjective. For instance, a gifted student might feel like a failure if he or she does not top the class, while a less academically inclined student might celebrate getting a passing grade.

When we face failure, it can be disheartening at first. But failure is not the end – it is an opportunity to learn and grow. Each failure teaches us valuable lessons and helps us improve.

History is full of examples of people who turned their failures into success.

Sumita Ghose faced a personal and professional setback when her husband, a development worker, was killed while working in a conflict zone. Determined to continue his legacy, Ghose founded Rang Sutra, a social enterprise aimed at providing sustainable livelihoods for rural artisans. Her initial efforts were met with scepticism and financial difficulties. However, through persistence and community engagement, she built a successful business that empowers thousands of artisans across India. This story is an example of turning personal tragedy into a mission for social good.

Arianna Huffington's journey is a testament to rising from failures. Her second book faced rejection from 36 publishers, highlighting the challenges she encountered early in her career.

Despite this setback, Huffington persisted and later transitioned into politics, running for governor of California state in the USA in 2003. Although her campaign received just 0.55 percent of the vote, this experience provided valuable insights, particularly in utilising the internet for fundraising, as she later acknowledged in a 2010 interview with *SUCCESS* magazine.

Huffington's entrepreneurial spirit and adaptability eventually led to the founding of *The Huffington Post,* a groundbreaking online news platform. The success of *The Huffington Post* underscored her ability to harness the power of digital media and adapt to changing trends in journalism. Additionally, Arianna has authored and published 13 books to date.

Failures humble us and make us more accepting of our limitations. They remind us that setbacks are a part of the journey to success. Instead of fearing failure, we should embrace it as an opportunity for growth. Success often arises from failure, and by learning from our mistakes, we can achieve our goals.

Embracing failures is essential for personal and professional growth. This mindset shift transforms challenges into stepping stones, leading to a growth-oriented approach to life. By acknowledging and embracing our failures, we not only build character but also inspire those around us to adopt a similar perspective.

Golden Rule:

View failures and setbacks as opportunities for growth and success.

#9 | LIVE IN THE PRESENT MOMENT

During my corporate tenure in the energy sector, I happened to attend one of the annual coal conferences with my friend in Bali, Indonesia. We were put up in an exotic resort by Nusa Dua beach.

We had some time off and we wanted to relax after a hectic schedule. My friend opted for the most extravagant spa treatment the resort had to offer, while I chose to relax on the beach, sipping a drink and reading a book.

After about an hour, my friend returned from his spa session, but he looked stressed.

"Was the spa experience not up to your expectation?" I asked him.

He said, "No. It was fantastic! Why do you ask that?"

"Because you look stressed, my friend."

"You guessed it right. While I was enjoying the spa, a thought suddenly crossed my mind, 'What if the coal prices plummet tomorrow?' The mere prospect of potential losses hijacked my peace of mind, and I could not relax," he said.

Just the thought of a probable event in the future ruined my friend's spa experience in the present. Our mind continuously wavers. We often find ourselves dwelling in the anger, guilt, regrets, and resentments of the past, or consumed by the fears and insecurities of the future. We spend our days caught in the web of virtual time, missing out on the beauty and opportunities of the present moment.

Here is an interesting yet profound concept. Time can be categorised into two types – *real time* and *virtual time.*

Living in the 'now' is living in the *real time* of the present, as life happens only in the present moment. It is the doorway to our highest success, goals, and potential. Living mindfully in the present enhances our ability to appreciate life's simple joys and find contentment.

Living in the past prevents us from fully experiencing and enjoying the present. Dwelling on past mistakes or regrets can lead to feelings of sadness, guilt, and hopelessness, hindering personal growth and happiness. It can also keep us trapped in old patterns, preventing us from embracing new opportunities and relationships. So, if you are living in the negative emotions of the past, then you are living in the *virtual time* of the past, as the past exists only in our memories.

Similarly, living in the future often breeds fears and insecurities, as it involves worrying about events that may never happen. This constant anticipation can lead to anxiety, making it difficult to enjoy the present. We might feel overwhelmed by potential challenges and uncertainties, lowering our confidence and sense of control. By fixating on the future, we miss out on the joy and opportunities of the present moment, ultimately hampering our ability to lead a balanced and happy life. So, if you are living with the fears and insecurities of the future, you are living in the *virtual time* of the future, as the future exists only in our imagination.

But what about the wisdom and lessons we can gain from the past? What about the happy memories that rejuvenate us? When we reflect on past experiences, we can identify patterns in our behaviour, understand our strengths and weaknesses, and gain valuable insights. This allows us to make more informed choices, avoid repeating mistakes, and build on our successes. Embracing lessons from the past – to become more resilient, wise, and better equipped – helps us to navigate challenges in the present. When we draw upon the positive experiences and knowledge of the past, we are still living in the *real time* of the past.

On the same lines, setting meaningful goals and creating actionable steps to achieve them helps in creating a meaningful and happy future. When we start identifying what truly brings us joy, we can prioritise these aspects in our present plans. By creating a roadmap and regularly reviewing it, we stay aligned with our growing ambitions. So, when we plan and prepare for our future, we are actively living in the *real time* of the future.

We must engage ourselves more in *real time* and less in *virtual time* to live in the present moment. **The present is where we have the power to make changes, take action, and create the life we desire.** It is where we can experience true joy, love, and fulfilment.

Living in the present means being fully present with ourselves and those around us. We embrace the beauty of each passing second and savour the richness of every experience. We let go of worries about the future and regrets from the past. We immerse ourselves in the task at hand, cherish the conversations we have, and relish the small moments of happiness that often go unnoticed.

Living in the 'now' requires practice and mindfulness. It means learning to quiet the noise in our minds and being fully attentive. We can cultivate this practice through meditation, deep breathing exercises, and by consciously bringing our attention back to the present whenever our thoughts wander.

In the present moment, we discover the untapped potential within us and unlock the door to our highest achievements. Life becomes more vibrant, meaningful, and fulfilling.

Golden Rule:

Living in the present moment is the key to a happy and successful life.

#10 | BE THE KINDEST PERSON YOU HAVE EVER MET

In one of the relief camps during the second World War, a nurse guided an exhausted, anxious soldier to the bedside of an elderly gentleman. "Your son is here," she softly announced to the old man. She had to repeat herself a few times before the patient's eyes fluttered open. He was heavily sedated due to the pain from his heart condition, but he faintly discerned the young soldier in uniform standing by the oxygen tent. With effort, he extended his hand.

The soldier gently clasped the old man's frail fingers, offering a silent reassurance of love and support. A chair was brought for him to sit, and throughout the night, he remained there, holding the old man's hand, and offering words of comfort and strength. Despite the nurse's occasional suggestion to take a break and rest, he steadfastly refused.

Intermittently, the nurse overheard him speaking softly. The elderly man, though fading, held onto his son's presence all through the night. As dawn approached, the old man passed away. The soldier released the lifeless hand he had been holding and went to inform the nurse. While she attended to her duties, he patiently waited for her return.

When she came back, preparing to offer words of condolence, the soldier interrupted her. "Who was that man?" he inquired.

"He was your father," she replied gently.

"No, he wasn't," the soldier responded firmly. "I've never met him before."

Surprised, the nurse asked, "Then why didn't you say anything when I led you to him?"

"I knew right away there had been a mix-up," he explained. "But I also knew he needed his son, and his son wasn't here. Even though he was too unwell to recognise me, I stayed because I knew how much he needed me."

The soldier's act of kindness was a genuine display of compassion and empathy towards a fellow human being in need. Sometimes, merely being there for someone, offering your presence and support, is the most meaningful thing you can do.

Kindness is a remarkable virtue. **When we practise kindness, we become instruments of the universe, serving and helping others.** It makes us more humble, sensitive, empathetic, and ultimately, better individuals. We must always try to give generously with love and compassion, without any expectation of reciprocation. If we are kind to others, the universe will show kindness to us in return, often manifold times over.

Golden Rule:

Be the kindest person you have ever encountered, offering compassion and support without any expectation.

#11 | GIVE HOPE TO OTHERS

In a groundbreaking study conducted by Curt Richter in the 1950s, researchers sought to understand the effects of hope on endurance. The experiment involved placing mice in a container of water and observing how long they would swim before giving up.

Mice were placed individually in jars filled with water. These jars were designed in such a way that the mice could not climb out, forcing them to keep swimming. The researchers observed that, on an average, the mice would give up and sink after about 15 minutes, succumbing to the apparent hopelessness of their situation.

In the second part of the experiment, Richter introduced a critical variable – hope. Just before the mice reached the point of exhaustion and began to drown, the researchers would temporarily rescue them, drying them off and giving them a brief period of rest before placing them back in the water.

Astonishingly, the mice that experienced this brief intervention swam for significantly longer periods when placed back in the water – often for hours or even days. The key difference was that these mice had experienced a moment of hope. They had learnt that the situation was not entirely hopeless and that rescue was possible.

The results of this experiment highlight the profound impact that hope can have on endurance and resilience. When the mice believed that there was a possibility of rescue, they were able to push beyond their previous limits and continue swimming much longer than those who had no such experience.

Just as the mice swam longer when they had hope, humans are more likely to persevere through difficult times when they believe that a positive outcome is possible. **Hope provides the psychological stamina needed to endure hardships.**

Small measures – whether it is a kind word, a helping hand, a moment of relief, or simply a hug – can significantly boost a person's hope and resilience. These moments can serve as powerful reminders that adversity is not permanent and that support is available.

By creating an environment where people can see possibilities beyond their current struggles, we can help them build and maintain hope. Encouraging a hopeful mindset can lead to greater perseverance and success in overcoming challenges. Family, friends, mentors, and community members can play a critical role in offering the encouragement and support needed to sustain hope.

The act of giving hope is a profound gift that costs nothing but means everything. By spreading hope, we can lift others from their despair and inspire them to find the strength within themselves to carry on with life's challenges.

Remember, each one of us has the power to give hope. We can be the beacon of light that someone needs to find their way out of the darkness. Never underestimate the impact you can have by simply being there, offering hope, and spreading love.

Golden Rule:

Give hope to others to empower them and light their way through challenges.

#12 | NEVER JUDGE OTHERS

Like most Indians, the game of cricket has always been my passion. I used to play regularly in my school and while in college. Then there was a long gap due to more pressing things in life and career. When I first joined my current cricket team Daring Dozen, thanks to my close friend Sunil Paaji (as he is fondly addressed), I felt a bit sceptical. This was no ordinary team. It was filled with actors and models, and ex-cricketers. Given their celebrity status, I thought they would be high-headed and not easy to gel with. Coming from a completely different field, I was apprehensive about being accepted as a team member. Adding to my anxiety was the fact that these players played regularly, while I had not been active on the field for a while. The idea of fitting in seemed daunting, and I felt intimidated.

Despite my doubts, I decided to give it a try. On my first day, I arrived at the practice session with a sense of unease. The team welcomed me with friendly smiles and warm greetings, but I could not shake off my initial apprehension. However, as the days went by, I began to see a different side of them.

During one of our matches, I finally got a chance to bat. I was nervous but when I scored my first runs, the entire team erupted in cheers. Their genuine enthusiasm and support took me by surprise. They went all out, appreciating my effort and making me feel like an integral part of the team. The captain even gifted me his personal cap.

One of the team members approached me after the game. Noticing my interest in creating YouTube videos and managing social media, he generously offered to help me with my projects.

Their friendly attitude and encouraging spirit completely shattered my preconceived notions about them.

As the weeks turned into months, I realised how wrong I had been to judge them. These individuals, whom I had initially thought would be aloof and egocentric, turned out to be incredibly warm and supportive. They effortlessly made me a part of their family, offering encouragement both on and off the field. This experience not only enhanced my cricket skills but also enriched my life with new lifetime friendships and deep meaningful connections.

We often judge those around us based on our own perspectives shaped by our personal experiences, fears, failures, and others' expectations and opinions. However, these judgements often lack logical grounding and may require periodic re-evaluation. **Each individual is on their unique journey, and without stepping into their shoes, we cannot fully comprehend**

their experiences, upbringing, or motivations for their behaviour. Therefore, passing judgement is a significant error on our part.

To overcome this tendency, we must remove the biased lenses through which we view others, and strive to see each person as they truly are. Acting with empathy, kindness, and compassion allows us to seek understanding rather than passing judgement. This approach benefits us in two ways: firstly, it enables us to perceive individuals more accurately, and secondly, it strengthens our relationships by developing deeper understanding and empathy.

We must focus on recognising the positive qualities in others rather than dwelling on our preconceived judgements. Here are a few tips on how not to judge others:

- Acknowledge that everyone has biases. Reflect on your own and how they may influence your judgements.
- Try to understand the other person's perspective, experiences, and motivations.
- Instead of making assumptions, ask questions to learn more about the person's situation.
- Look for common ground and shared interests rather than focusing on differences.
- Remember that everyone has a unique story, struggles, and aspirations.

- Focus on people's positive qualities and strengths rather than their shortcomings.
- Accept that everyone is different and that these differences do not equate to being better or worse.
- Accept people as they are, recognising that everyone is on their own journey.
- Pay attention to what others are saying without interrupting or forming judgements mid-conversation.
- Approach conversations with an open mind, ready to accept new ideas and perspectives.

With conscious effort, you can cultivate a more empathetic, understanding, and non-judgemental approach to interacting with others.

Golden Rule:

By accepting everyone as they are and focusing on their positive qualities, we not only enhance our relationships but also contribute to a more harmonious and inclusive environment.

#13 | ACCEPTANCE IS A GREAT VIRTUE

In a small coastal village by the Mediterranean Sea, there lived an experienced fisherman named Moshe. For years, Moshe had been respected for his firm dedication to his vocation. His fishing trips were meticulously planned, relying on his deep knowledge of tides and weather patterns to ensure successful catches. Moshe took immense pride in his ability to control his outcomes, a trait that defined his identity and earned him respect among his peers.

However, one summer, the weather patterns began to shift unpredictably. Storms materialised out of nowhere, and the once-reliable tides became erratic. Despite his best efforts, Moshe frequently returned to shore empty-handed. Frustration and anxiety began to get the better of him. He cursed the sea, regretting his lost sense of control.

One stormy day, Moshe came across an elderly sailor named Jonah, a man who had spent his entire life navigating the sea. Jonah's calm temperament in the face of the storm puzzled Moshe. Desperate for advice, Moshe approached Jonah and asked him how he managed to remain so serene despite the unpredictable nature of the open seas.

Jonah smiled warmly and shared his wisdom: "The sea is a force beyond our control. It has its own rhythms and whims. Fighting against it only brings frustration. Acceptance, on the other hand, brings peace. When you accept the sea for what it is, you learn to work with it, not against it. This is where true wisdom lies."

Intrigued, Moshe decided to give acceptance a try. Instead of rigidly sticking to his plans, he began to observe the sea from a new perspective. He learnt to read its subtle cues and adapted his methods accordingly. If the sea was too rough, he would mend his nets or assist other fishermen instead of battling the waves.

Over time, Moshe noticed a profound change within himself. By accepting the sea's unpredictability, he became more patient and resilient. He discovered new fishing spots he had previously overlooked and even found joy in the simple act of being on the water, regardless of the catch. His wisdom grew, not from controlling the sea, but from understanding, respecting and accepting its nature.

Moshe's transformation was gradual but remarkable. His once-rigid mindset softened, and his frustration melted away. He found a sense of peace and contentment he had never experienced before. Acceptance had unlocked a deeper connection with the sea, allowing him to navigate its challenges with grace and wisdom.

Moshe's newfound acceptance extended beyond his fishing. He became more compassionate and understanding towards others. He learnt to accept people's differences and saw value in their unique perspectives. His relationships improved, and he became a pillar of support for those around him. Acceptance had not only made Moshe a better fisherman but also a better person.

Like the sea, life is often unpredictable too. We often face situations that are beyond our control. This can be due to a variety of factors such as complexity of nature, human behaviour, random events, evolution and change, our health, and unforeseen challenges. Unpredictability is an inherent part of the human experience. It challenges us to adapt, grow, and find meaning amidst the uncertainty.

On the other hand, the instinct to resist and fight against uncertainty leads to frustration and unhappiness. When we do not accept life as it is, several negative consequences can arise. Constantly struggling to control or change the uncontrollable aspects of life can lead to heightened stress and anxiety, strained relationships, and loss of joy. It may result in decreased creativity, limiting our ability to see new possibilities, and continued dissatisfaction, finally affecting our physical and mental health.

Moshe's story illustrates the profound virtue of acceptance. **Acceptance allows us to find peace amidst chaos and become wiser.** It teaches us patience, adaptability, and empathy. By embracing the volatility of life, we can discover a profound inner peace and a deeper connection with the world.

Acceptance is not about resignation or passivity. It is about understanding the nature of things and adapting to them with grace. It is about recognising our limitations and finding strength in our ability to navigate through uncertainty. Acceptance teaches us to let go of our need for control and to embrace the beauty of life's randomness.

With acceptance, we become more compassionate and understanding, both towards ourselves and others. We learn to appreciate the uniqueness of every situation and every individual.

Acceptance is a great virtue that can transform our lives in profound ways. It shows us the pathway to inner peace, wisdom, and contentment.

Golden Rule:

Accept the unpredictability of life, and find peace and wisdom in adapting to its ever-changing nature.

#14 | CHOOSE WISELY

In ancient India, there lived a revered teacher named Mrugacharya, known throughout the land for his unmatched skill in swordsmanship and his wisdom. Many princes and warriors sought his guidance to master the art of the sword.

One day, two young princes, Purastya and Nrup, approached Mrugacharya, seeking to become his disciples. The teacher accepted them and began their rigorous training. After several years of intense practice, Mrugacharya decided it was time for the princes to choose their swords, a crucial decision that would shape their futures.

Mrugacharya presented them with two options: a beautifully adorned sword with intricate carvings and a plain-looking but perfectly balanced sword. He advised them to choose wisely, as their choice would greatly affect their journey as warriors.

Purastya, captivated by the beauty of the decorative sword, chose it without hesitation. Nrup, however, took his time, weighed the options, and chose the plain-looking sword, valuing its balance and craftsmanship over its appearance.

Years passed, and both princes continued their training under Mrugacharya's guidance. Purastya, though talented, often struggled with his sword, finding it cumbersome and difficult to wield in intense battles. Its beauty had no bearing on its effectiveness, and Purastya's progress was stuck.

Nrup, on the other hand, excelled with his plain sword. Its perfect balance allowed him to master advanced techniques and fight with precision and ease. He became a formidable warrior, surpassing Purastya and earning respect and recognition throughout the kingdom.

One day, during a grand tournament, Purastya faced Nrup in the final match. Despite his best efforts, Purastya was outmatched, and Nrup's wise choice of sword proved to be a decisive factor in his victory.

After the match, Mrugacharya approached Purastya and said, "You see, Purastya, the choice of your sword was a reflection of your priorities. In life, just as in battle, decisions often present themselves as a choice between immediate allure and lasting value. We must choose wisely, looking beyond superficial attraction and valuing what truly matters. By prioritising substance over appearance and making informed decisions, we set ourselves on a path to true greatness." Purastya learnt a valuable lesson that day.

Choice is a powerful gift we receive from the moment we are born. It is our right, and we should use it wisely. Every choice we make shapes our path and affects how quickly we reach our goals.

Our choices can either bring us closer to our purpose or take us away from it. If we think of our life as a graph, each choice is a dot that marks our direction. At every moment, we can choose to move towards our goals or away from them. The pattern of our choices shows the path our life is taking.

Remember, we always have the freedom to change our direction. If we realise we are off-course, we can choose to correct it. This power to choose lets us shape our future.

Living consciously means taking responsibility for our actions and decisions. It means designing our life rather than leaving it to chance. It means making changes instead of making excuses, seeking motivation instead of falling for manipulation, and striving for excellence instead of competing unfairly.

Our choices also affect our thoughts and emotions. We can choose to act from anger or from love and compassion. Anger builds walls that isolate us, while compassion builds bridges that connect us.

We can choose between fear and courage. Fear limits us, while courage pushes us forward.

We can choose faith over doubt. Faith brings peace and understanding, while doubt brings frustration and regret.

Choosing self-esteem over self-pity affects how we see ourselves and the world.

Forgiveness instead of blame frees us from resentment and brings compassion and peace.

Acceptance over resistance helps us move forward by acknowledging things we cannot change. What we resist will persist.

By using our power of choice, we shape our future. Our lives are not just controlled by what happens to us but by how we choose to respond. Through deliberate choices, we align with our purpose and navigate life with intention and grace.

Our power to choose is a profound gift, one that can change our direction at any moment. By making conscious, thoughtful decisions, we take control of our destiny, turning aspirations into achievements and dreams into reality. Accepting the responsibility that comes with our choices enables us to create a life that reflects our true purpose and values.

Golden Rule:

Choose wisely, with courage and compassion, for in these choices lies the blueprint of your future.

#15 | QUESTION ESTABLISHED BELIEFS AND PATTERNS

We go through conditioning from the time we are born. Our language, class, religion, life patterns, belief systems, and even the meaning of wealth and success are handed down to us. We are taught what it means to be a part of a region, a community, and what we should or should not do in life. These beliefs and patterns shape our existence, and we unknowingly base our lives upon them.

However, little do we realise that these very beliefs could be limiting us from reaching our true potential and achieving our life goals.

The conditioning we receive etches in us the idea that what others say about us or about life is true, while our own dreams hold no significant meaning. We begin to live solely for the approval and acceptance of others, unaware that we are distancing ourselves from our authentic selves. These firmly established beliefs become the guiding principles in our decision-making processes and are deeply ingrained in our collective consciousness. We start assuming that these beliefs are unchanging and unalterable, leaving no room for growth or transformation.

Nevertheless, it is essential for our personal growth to periodically question these established beliefs and patterns. By doing so, we open ourselves up to new perspectives and insights. **When we challenge these beliefs, we grant ourselves the opportunity to tap into our potential and pursue our own dreams.**

History is full of examples of people who went against established norms to say what was right.

Galileo Galilei, a pioneering physicist, mathematician, and astronomer, played a pivotal role in reshaping our understanding of the cosmos during the 17th century. At that time, the prevailing belief was that the Earth was the centre of the universe, with celestial bodies orbiting around it.

Using a newly invented telescope, Galileo made groundbreaking observations that challenged the geocentric model. His findings provided compelling evidence for Copernicus's heliocentric theory, which suggested that the Earth and planets orbit the Sun.

Galileo's heliocentric model brought him into direct conflict with the Church, which viewed his theory as contradicting religious doctrine. In 1616, he was cautioned by the Church to refrain from declaring heliocentrism as fact. Despite these warnings, Galileo persisted and in 1632, he published his work presenting arguments in favour of heliocentrism.

This publication led to Galileo's trial in 1633, where he was charged with dissent for his beliefs. He had to spend the rest of his life under house arrest. Despite this harassment, his work laid the groundwork for the eventual acceptance of Copernican theory and profoundly influenced the development of modern astronomy.

Galileo Galilei's life exemplifies the courage to challenge established beliefs and question prevailing scientific and religious orthodoxy, despite personal risk.

Questioning established beliefs helps us break free from societal constraints and embrace our individuality. When we challenge the patterns that have shaped our lives, we start a journey of self-discovery and empowerment. This exploration allows us to understand our true desires and aspirations without being limited by others' expectations.

Remember, you do not have to believe everything that is told to you about yourself, the world and the 'right' or 'normal' way to do things. These norms have also been created by humans like us. And there can always be a possibility of a shortcoming or a mistake in their perception. Moreover, perceptions about life and how to live life successfully are subjective and can change from person to person, place to place, and time to time.

False narratives have been created time and again by people who wished to rule over others. These have deeply impacted culture and traditions all over the world. The fact is that if a false statement is repeated over and over again, and it is accepted as the truth by more than two people, it becomes a norm. If it is a norm maintained over many generations, it becomes a tradition.

We humans are supposedly the most intelligent species on the planet. We have the free will and discernment to choose the information fed to us in the name of tradition, and to not follow blindly. We must encourage critical thinking, question assumptions and seek diverse perspectives.

Following a set pattern is like walking on the beaten path. You will never know what you could otherwise achieve if you had followed your heart. When you question a set belief or norm, you have a possibility of unlearning the old and learning something new. You also give yourself a chance to chart your own course of life, and create a completely new path for yourself.

By re-evaluating deeply ingrained beliefs, you can redefine success, happiness, and fulfilment on your own terms. You begin to see that your dreams are significant. This self-inquiry helps to shed societal conditioning, letting you express your authentic self.

Challenging established beliefs requires courage and an open mind. It means being willing to question the status quo and embrace uncertainty. However, one thing is certain. Through this introspection, you can overcome your limitations and fears to unlock your highest potential.

Golden Rule:

Questioning established beliefs liberates us from societal conditioning and empowers us to pursue our true potential.

#16 BELIEVE IN YOURSELF AND YOUR ABILITIES

Once, a farmer found an abandoned eagle's nest with a warm egg inside. He brought it back to his farm and placed it among the hen's eggs.

When the eggs hatched, the baby eagle grew up with the chickens. He lived its whole life pecking grain in the farmyard. One day, when he was old, he happened to look up. He saw a magnificent sight. High above in the blue sky, there was an eagle flying majestically. He sighed and said to himself, "If only I was born an eagle."

Just like the eagle, we all have unique qualities and abilities. But as we grow, we forget about this and start believing what others say about us. We need to break free from social conditioning and discover our uniqueness. Only then will the world see our true selves.

Believing in yourself and your abilities is a key to success. Reflect on your talents, skills, and positive qualities, and embrace your weaknesses by viewing them as opportunities for growth rather than as flaws. Visualise achieving your goals and overcoming challenges, then take action by starting with small steps to build confidence with each achievement. Understand that setbacks are part of the journey and use them as learning experiences.

Have faith in your capabilities and dreams, even when faced with doubts. Remember, no one is perfect, and we are all bound to make mistakes. Do not let your mistakes and failures create doubts about yourself. Never believe in others' opinions about you, as people may say things that stop you from moving ahead or create doubts in your mind. Do not listen to them; **you do not need to believe everything that is said about you. Discount your critics.**

Get out of societal conditioning, which often makes us form limiting beliefs. You are expected to live life in a set pattern, and if you do not follow, you are labelled a rebel. Embrace your uniqueness and trust in your path. By believing in yourself, identifying your strengths, accepting your weaknesses, and taking action despite doubts and societal pressures, you can accomplish great things and live up to your full potential.

You are unique and there is no one like you in the entire universe.

Golden Rule:

Identify and believe in your uniqueness and true power, and never doubt your potential for greatness.

#17 | BE COURAGEOUS

Courage is standing up for something you believe in, or standing by your values when you have an easier option out.

Many tales of courage were witnessed during the Covid pandemic. Doctors, nurses and the medical workers showed extraordinary courage, going out of their way to save patients. Their selfless, courageous acts helped avert many Covid casualties.

During the second surge, the doctors who were exhausted and overworked both physically and emotionally showed amazing resilience, strength, and creativity in the face of this despair and devastation. Some of the physicians I personally knew worked tirelessly, often with minimum gear to protect themselves, long shift hours, and heightened risk of infection. Not only did they go through the anxiety of being separated from their families, some were even unable to see their children for many weeks, and also endured social banishment.

All these health workers had an easy option out, but they chose to stand up for their values. That is true courage.

Courage is not about insane bravery. It is simply about having the guts to let go of personal security or comfort because someone else is in dire need. The value of our lives is not measured by what we do for ourselves, but by what we do for others.

There is an inspiring story of a boy named Riyaz whose act of courage is incredible.

In 2003, nine-year-old Riyaz found himself playing near a park in Dollyganj, Lucknow, just a few years older than a five-year-old girl who stood dangerously close to the rail tracks. As a train hurtled towards her, Riyaz cried out, desperately trying to warn her of the impending danger. However, his shouts were drowned out by the chaos of the surroundings. Even his father, who was nearby, remained unaware of the approaching train.

With no time to spare, Riyaz dashed towards the girl, acting on pure instinct. Ignoring his own safety, he managed to pull her to safety just as the train thundered past. However, in his heroic efforts to save her, Riyaz found himself trapped on the tracks, and the train's momentum led to the crushing of his two arms and one leg.

Despite the harrowing ordeal, Riyaz's selfless actions saved the girl's life. Following extensive medical treatment, he eventually recovered, his courage standing as a testament to the indomitable spirit of human kindness and sacrifice.

Courage manifests in various forms, from the quiet courage of ordinary people facing everyday hardships, to

the bold acts of heroism that capture the world's attention. It can be found in the single parent working multiple jobs to provide for their family, the activist speaking out against injustice, or the firefighter rushing into a burning building to save lives.

In 1955, Montgomery, Alabama, was deeply segregated, with public buses divided into sections for white and black passengers. On December 1, 1955, after a long day of work, 42-year-old Rosa Parks took a seat in the "coloured" section of a bus. As more passengers boarded and the "white" section filled up, the bus driver demanded that Rosa and three other black passengers give up their seats for a white man. While the others complied, Rosa firmly refused. She was arrested for violating the city's segregation laws, but her act of defiance was a calculated stand against the injustices she had long witnessed.

Rosa's arrest sparked the Montgomery Bus Boycott, led by a then-unknown pastor named Martin Luther King Jr. For 381 days, African-Americans refused to ride the city buses, severely impacting the bus company's finances, and drawing national attention to the civil-rights struggle. The boycott eventually led to a Supreme Court ruling that segregation on public buses was unconstitutional. Rosa Parks' courage and quiet strength became a pivotal moment in the American Civil Rights Movement, demonstrating that one person's stand against injustice can indeed make a significant difference.

Courage is not confined to grand gestures or extraordinary circumstances. It permeates the fabric of everyday life. It is found in the small acts of kindness, compassion, and integrity that shape our interactions with others and define our character. It is the courage to speak up for what is right, saying 'No' when needed, asking for what is rightfully yours, being honest and truthful when there is an easier option, taking responsibility for your actions, lending a helping hand to those in need, forgiving easily, loving unconditionally, and persevering in the face of setbacks and adversity.

Courage is also deeply intertwined with vulnerability, as it requires individuals to expose themselves to the possibility of danger, failure, rejection, or criticism. It is the willingness to embrace vulnerability as a source of strength rather than weakness, recognising that true courage lies in authenticity and resilience.

In the face of uncertainty and doubt, courage offers us a guiding light, illuminating the path forward and instilling within us the confidence to pursue our dreams and aspirations. It is a guiding light in times of darkness, reminding us of our innate capacity for growth, resilience, and greatness.

Golden Rule:

Stand tall and be courageous in the face of difficulties and challenges, even if you may have an easier option.

#18 | BE PATIENT

Tokyo has a reputation of being a busy metropolitan city, filled with towering, modern skyscrapers. Yet amidst these structures, several beautiful gardens add a touch of natural beauty to this dynamic urban landscape.

One such serene community garden was tended by an elderly man named Hiroshi Tanaka. Hiroshi had been a gardener all his life, and his expertise showed in the lush, vibrant plants that thrived under his care. The garden was a haven of tranquillity amidst the city's chaos, attracting visitors who came to admire its beauty and find a moment of peace.

One spring, a young man named Kenji moved into the neighbourhood. Kenji was ambitious and always in a hurry, eager to achieve success in his new job and in life. One day, while jogging past the garden, he noticed Hiroshi carefully planting seeds. Intrigued by the garden's beauty, Kenji decided to stop and chat.

"How do you make this garden so beautiful?" Kenji asked.

Hiroshi smiled and replied, "Patience. Every plant takes time to grow. You can't rush nature."

Kenji scoffed inwardly. He had always believed that success came from pushing hard and moving fast. But he decided to humour the old man and volunteered to help in the garden during his free time, thinking he might learn something useful.

Weeks passed, and Kenji became increasingly frustrated. He had planted seeds alongside Hiroshi, but he saw no immediate results. "Why aren't they growing faster?" he complained.

Hiroshi chuckled softly. "Some things can't be rushed, Kenji san. They need time to take root, to absorb the nutrients from the soil, and to grow strong."

Kenji found it hard to accept this slow process. However, as the weeks turned into months, he began to notice subtle changes. The seeds he had planted were sprouting, and the sprouts were slowly growing into sturdy plants. He realised that the garden required not only patience but also consistent care and attention.

One day, a particular plant caught Kenji's eye. It was the plant of a rare flower that Hiroshi had been nurturing for years. Hiroshi explained that this flower only bloomed once every five years, but when it did, its beauty was unparalleled. Kenji was sceptical but decided to keep an eye on it.

As time went on, Kenji's attitude began to change. The process of tending to the garden became a form of meditation for him. He started to find joy in the small, incremental progress of the plants. His patience grew, and with it, his understanding of the natural rhythms of life.

One morning, almost five years after Kenji had first planted the seed of the rare flower, he walked into the garden and was greeted by the sight of the flower in full bloom. It was breathtakingly beautiful, more than he had ever imagined. Hiroshi stood beside him, smiling.

"See, Kenji? Patience brings rewards that haste cannot. This garden is a testament to that."

Kenji felt a deep sense of contentment. He realised that his impatience had often blinded him to the beauty of gradual progress and the satisfaction of steady, patient effort. The lesson he learnt in the garden began to influence other aspects of his life. He became more patient at work, more understanding in his relationships, and more appreciative of the slow unfolding of life. In the heart of the bustling city, Hiroshi's garden stood as a living reminder of the virtue of patience. It taught everyone who visited that true growth, whether in plants or in life, requires time, care, and above all, patience.

Patience is a virtue often overlooked in our fast-paced world. We live in an age where instant gratification is the norm, and the value of slow, steady progress is often forgotten. Rushing the process often leads to frustration and disappointment. Instead, when we approach our goals with patience, we allow ourselves the necessary time to grow, learn, and adapt.

In our daily lives, patience can manifest in various ways. It might be the patience to listen fully to someone without interrupting, the patience to wait for the right opportunity rather than forcing a decision, or the patience to allow ourselves to make mistakes and learn from them.

Patience teaches us to appreciate the journey rather than just the destination. It helps us remain calm in the face of adversity, understanding that challenges are a part of the growth process. By cultivating patience, we develop resilience and the ability to navigate life's ups and downs with grace.

The virtue of patience also has a ripple effect on our relationships. When we are patient with others, we create an environment of understanding and compassion. We give people the space to express themselves and grow at their own pace. This, in turn, strengthens our connections and builds trust.

In the workplace, patience can lead to better teamwork and collaboration. When we are patient with our colleagues, we create a supportive atmosphere that encourages creativity and innovation. We recognise that great ideas often take time to develop and that setbacks are opportunities for learning.

To embrace patience is to embrace the natural flow of life. It is to understand that some things cannot be rushed and that true growth takes time. By practising patience, we allow ourselves to be present in each moment, appreciating the journey and the lessons it brings.

As the Zen saying goes, "Patience is the road to wisdom." Let us walk this road with calm and steady steps, trusting that each moment of patience brings us closer to our true selves and our ultimate goals.

Golden Rule:

Embrace patience to appreciate the journey, build resilience, and create understanding in a fast-paced world.

#19 | PAUSE BEFORE YOU ACT

In the ancient Chinese kingdom of Shengdao, there was a respected general named Li Huang who led his troops with wisdom and courage. His strategic mind and calm conduct in any situation earned him the admiration and loyalty of his soldiers. However, even the greatest leaders are tested by their own emotions.

Once, Li Huang and his army were fighting a battle far from their homeland against a neighbouring kingdom to expand their territory. One evening, after a gruelling battle, Li Huang received news that his homeland Shengdao had been attacked by a rival kingdom. Exhausted from the day's fight, his body ached, and his mind was clouded with fatigue. He felt a deep, simmering anger towards the enemies who dared to invade his beloved country. Anxiety and loneliness crept into his heart as he thought of his family back home, potentially in danger.

Driven by his raw emotions, General Li Huang called his advisors and ordered an immediate counterattack. His advisors, seeing his state, hesitated but followed his command out of loyalty and fear of his wrath. The troops, equally exhausted and demoralised, marched towards the enemy's stronghold in the dead of night.

The enemy, however, was well-rested and prepared. The hasty counterattack led to a devastating defeat, with many soldiers lost and the general himself narrowly escaping capture. It was a bitter lesson for Li Huang. His rash decision, made in a moment of hurt, anger, anxiety, loneliness, and fatigue, cost him dearly.

In the aftermath, as he recovered and reflected on his actions, Li Huang vowed never to let his emotions dictate his decisions again.

In moments of emotional turmoil, our judgement can be clouded, leading to decisions we might regret later. Taking the time to rest and reflect can often provide the clarity needed to make better choices.

Never take an important decision or make an important choice when you are Hurt, Angry, Lonely and Tired (HALT). Most often, a decision made during such times will go wrong or you will make a mess of the situation.

Reacting impulsively in these vulnerable states can lead to actions that are disproportionate and misguided. **Instead of immediately reacting, it is wise to pause and take a moment to gather your thoughts.** Stepping back, taking a few deep breaths, or finding a quiet space can help calm your emotions. Sipping water or having a cup of tea or simply going away from the situation will provide clarity.

By giving yourself this space to relax and regain composure, you are better able to make sound decisions and respond appropriately. It allows you to detach from the immediate inner chaos and approach the situation with a calmer demeanour. This clarity enables you to consider the consequences of your actions and choose a response that aligns with your values and intentions.

So, remember, do not react when you are Hurt, Angry, Lonely and Tired.

Golden Rule:

Pause and gather yourself before making decisions when you are Hurt, Angry, Lonely, and Tired (HALT) to avoid regrets later on.

#20 | HANG UP YOUR WORRIES

Once, when I was travelling to another city for work, my friend Ravi, who lived there, invited me over for dinner. He offered to pick me up from the hotel, and during our drive to his home, we shared stories about how our day had passed. As Ravi spoke, however, I noticed a sense of exasperation and worry in his voice.

He recounted how his day had been particularly challenging. A flat tyre had cost him precious time, causing him to lose an hour of work. On top of that, he mentioned losing a contract and facing the disappointment of his boss. It seemed like one of those days where everything went wrong.

We arrived at his house, and as we approached the front door, I noticed him briefly pause by a small tree, gently touching the tips of its branches with both hands as if hanging something.

As soon as we entered the house, I witnessed a remarkable transformation in Ravi. His previously strained expression was replaced by a radiant smile as he greeted his two small children and his wife with hugs. It was as if the weight of his worries had instantly lifted.

Curious about the tree outside, I asked Ravi about it. Smiling, he explained, "Oh, that's my trouble tree. I hang up my worries on it every night when I come home. Then in the morning, I pick them up again. But when I return to it in the morning to retrieve my worries, they often seemed to have reduced in number."

It was a simple yet profound practice that seemed to bring him peace in the middle of life's challenges.

Worrying is when we feel anxious or scared about things that might happen in the future. Worry stems from dwelling on uncertainties and potential negative outcomes, which can paralyse us and prevent us from fully experiencing the richness of life. It is like having a voice in our head that keeps telling us something bad is going to happen.

But worrying does not actually solve problems; it just makes us feel more stressed and upset. **We often imagine worse things happening to us in the future, which may not happen at all.** And the more we worry, the bigger our problems can seem in our mind.

But there are ways to deal with worry.

1. **Shift attention from fears and anxieties to the present moment, embracing life with openness and enthusiasm.** This means paying attention to what

is happening right now, rather than getting caught up in what might happen later. Living in the present also allows us to appreciate the small pleasures, build meaningful relationships, and pursue our passions with a sense of freedom.

2. **Accept that life is unpredictable and that bad things can happen sometimes.** Instead of trying to control everything, we can learn to adapt and find ways to cope with whatever comes our way.
3. **Facing our fears and being brave can also help.** Instead of avoiding the things that make us anxious, we can confront them and learn that we are stronger than we think.

With practice, we can start to worry less and enjoy life more, knowing that we have the power to handle whatever challenges come our way. We can free ourselves to engage more deeply with the world around us, enjoying the joys and opportunities that each day brings.

Hang your worries on the tree!

Golden Rule:

Leave your worries behind and find peace in the present moment.

#21 | GRATITUDE BRINGS HAPPINESS

In the highlands of Tibet, there lived a humble monk leading a simple life in a monastery. His day was filled with rituals and profound devotion. At the break of dawn, he rose to the soft clang of prayer bells. Clad in a saffron robe, he would then join his fellow monks in the courtyard for morning chants. Throughout the day, he would engage himself in tasks such as tending to the monastery gardens and studying scriptures. The day ended with a simple meal of rice and vegetables, eaten in reverent silence, and finally returning to his cell under the canopy of stars.

But despite studying many scriptures, and engaging in spiritual discourses, he could not find the secret of true happiness.

Once when he was wandering through the valleys and forests late in the day, he was caught in a sudden storm. While he was looking for shelter in a small village, an elderly woman named Tara welcomed him into her home with open arms.

Tara lived in a small, weather-beaten cottage on the outskirts of the village. Her home, constructed from mud and thatch, barely shielded her from the elements. Inside, she had a worn straw mat, few utensils, and an earthen stove where she cooked meals over an open fire. The flickering light of an oil lamp illuminated the humble space. Tara's face bore the gentle lines of wisdom and contentment. Despite having very little, she happily offered the monk a warm meal and a place to sleep.

In the morning, as the monk prepared to leave, he thanked Tara profusely for her kindness. Intrigued, he could not stop himself from asking her the secret of her happiness and contentment, despite having so little. She simply smiled and said, "Child, true happiness comes not from what we possess, but from the gratitude we carry in our hearts. I am grateful for every small thing I have been blessed with."

The monk finally got the answer he was looking for in scriptures. He realised that gratitude is the key to true happiness. It is not about having everything we desire, but appreciating what we already have – our breath, the sun's warmth, the beauty of nature, and the kindness of others.

After coming back to the quiet monastery garden, amidst the whispering winds and fluttering prayer flags, he sat in peaceful silence, grateful for the timeless wisdom that he had received on his journey toward true happiness.

Gratitude has the remarkable ability to cultivate happiness in our lives. When we adopt a mindset of gratitude, we shift our focus from what we lack to what we have, allowing us to appreciate the abundance that surrounds us. By acknowledging and expressing gratitude for our blessings, big and small, we invite joy and contentment into our hearts.

I am always grateful that I have been blessed with good health and opportunities for growth in my life. I am filled with gratitude for the opportunities given to me for helping and guiding those who feel stagnated or lost. And one of the key things that I am extremely thankful for is being able to look after my parents, till their final moments.

Gratitude encourages us to savour the present moment, finding beauty and meaning in everyday experiences. It creates a sense of connection with others and with the world around us, enriching our relationships. By practising gratitude, we open ourselves up to a profound sense of happiness that goes beyond external circumstances, enriching our lives in limitless ways.

We attract more of what we are grateful for. When we are grateful, we emit positive energy that attracts similar positive experiences. By appreciating what we have, we align ourselves with positive vibrations, which can help manifest our desires and make us more aware of opportunities.

Here are a few tips on practising gratitude:

- Keep a gratitude journal, and write down the things that you are grateful for in your life, however small they may seem. Make this a daily practice and revisit the list in your low moments.

— Take the time to thank people in your life, whether through a heartfelt note, a quick message, or a face-to-face conversation.

— Hang a sign on your door that says, "Be Grateful." Touch it every time you walk through the door.

— Discuss what you are grateful for with friends or family. This can enhance your relationships and spread positivity.

These simple practices can help create a positive mindset and environment, drawing more good things into your life. Cultivate gratitude in every moment, whether in times of abundance or adversity.

True happiness blossoms from within, rooted in a heart overflowing with gratitude for life's blessings, no matter how small.

Golden Rule:

Gratitude shifts our focus from what we lack to what we have, giving true happiness and enriching our lives with joy and contentment.

#22 | FIND JOY IN SIMPLE THINGS

We are blessed with a house that has a small terrace. My wife is passionate about gardening and she usually dedicates her Sunday mornings to her passion. One such morning, when she was working in the garden, she called out to me loudly, "Come here!" I left everything I was doing and rushed to see what had happened. My wife was jumping with excitement and joy. I was relieved to see that everything was okay, and asked her about the urgency of calling me. She grabbed my hand like a child, and pulled me to see the flowers that had bloomed on her rose plant. Practically speaking, it was just a bud blooming into a flower, but it brought so much of joy to my wife. These are the small joys of life.

When we go for our evening walks, we meet a street dog every day and as soon as he sees us, he starts wagging his tail and comes running towards us. We have named him Sparky. The unconditional love that we see in his eyes gives us immense joy.

Real joy is not found in extravagant gestures but in the simple moments of everyday life. It is about appreciating these little moments and finding happiness in the ordinary. Whether it is spending time with loved ones, laughing with friends, taking a leisurely walk in nature, savouring a favourite treat, or just sitting with a cup of tea and a book, all by yourself – these little moments remind us that life is meant to be enjoyed.

Often, in our pursuit of grand achievements or material possessions, we overlook the power of simplicity. We may believe that true happiness lies in reaching certain milestones or acquiring certain things. However, this mindset keeps us waiting for happiness, neglecting the joy readily available in the present moment.

Finding joy in the simple things does not require waiting for extraordinary events. It is about fully embracing the beauty of the here and now.

The pursuit of happiness should not hinge on achieving big goals. It should be in finding contentment in the present moment. By appreciating the beauty in the ordinary, we become more attuned to the blessings that surround us.

When we find joy in life's simple pleasures, we embrace the essence of life itself. Happiness becomes a journey rather than a destination, made up of countless small moments strung together. These simple joys act as anchors, grounding us in the present and reminding us of what truly matters.

Golden Rule:

True happiness lies in appreciating the simple joys and moments of everyday life.

#23 | CREATE DEEP MEANINGFUL RELATIONSHIPS

In today's hyper-connected world, it is easy to accumulate a large number of 'friends' and followers on social media. We measure our popularity by the number of likes and comments we receive, but we often overlook the importance of genuine connections. Having thousands of friends on social media may seem impressive, but it does not guarantee the presence of even a single person with whom we can truly connect.

Priya lived in the lively city of Mumbai, and was known for her vibrant social-media presence that attracted thousands of followers. She had a constant stream of likes and comments on her posts, which showcased her glamorous lifestyle, her travels, and her seemingly endless array of friends. Despite her popularity, Priya often felt a deep sense of loneliness. She spent evenings scrolling through her feeds, seeking connection in likes and comments that left her wanting.

One day, Priya received a message from her childhood friend,

Ayesha, inviting her to a small gathering with a few old schoolmates. Reluctant at first, Priya decided to join, hoping for a change from her virtual interactions.

The gathering took place at a cozy cafe in Bandra. As they recalled their school days and shared stories of their lives with candour and humour, Priya felt a warmth and authenticity that she had missed over the years. Ayesha and the others in the group spoke with honesty and openness, creating a bond that social media could not replicate. Their conversation swept through her otherwise pretentious and stagnant life like a breath of fresh air. Priya realised that amidst the superficiality of online connections, it was these genuine moments with old friends that filled her with joy and a sense of belonging.

She immediately decided to prioritise deeper relationships over virtual ones, finding fulfilment in the love and support of a few true friends. As Priya sat with Ayesha and their friends, watching the Mumbai skyline, she felt grateful for the real connections that brought her happiness beyond the screen. She understood that having two or three close friends who truly cared was far more valuable than thousands of virtual acquaintances.

True and deep meaningful relationships are built on trust, openness, and non-judgemental acceptance. These relationships cannot be formed overnight. They require time, effort, and emotional investment. In a world where instant gratification is the norm, nurturing such relationships may seem daunting, but the rewards are many.

Imagine having two or three individuals in your life whom you can trust implicitly, individuals who listen to you without judgement, who stand by you in times of adversity. These people may not solve all your problems or offer material help, but their unwavering support and understanding makes them invaluable.

Creating deep meaningful relationships is like planting seeds and watching them grow. It requires patience, care, and attention. We need to invest time and energy in knowing and understanding the people around us. Genuine connections are not superficial. They delve into the core of our being and help us feel truly seen and heard.

We live in times when money and possessions often define success, and it is easy to overlook the profound value of true friendship. Money can buy comfort and luxury, but it cannot buy the warmth and solace that comes from having someone who cares deeply about us. True friends are our true wealth, and they enrich our lives in ways that material possessions cannot.

Deep meaningful relationships provide us with a safe space where we can be our authentic selves. They offer a refuge from the pressures and expectations of the outside world. In these relationships, we find solace, understanding, and the strength to face life's challenges.

How to build deep and meaningful relationships?

Invest time and energy

Just like wealth, deep relationships require investment. This means dedicating time and energy to nurture these connections. Regular communication, spending quality time together, and showing genuine interest in each other's lives are crucial. It is through these interactions that trust and understanding are built, laying the foundation for an authentic and meaningful bond.

Be non-judgemental

To cultivate a relationship where you feel safe and accepted, it is essential to adopt a non-judgemental attitude. Avoid rushing to conclusions or passing judgement on your friend's actions or words. Instead, strive to understand their perspective and offer your support without criticism. This creates a safe space where both parties can express themselves freely, knowing they will not be judged.

Show empathy and understanding

Empathy is the cornerstone of deep relationships. It involves not only understanding but also feeling what the other person is going through. Being sensitive to their feelings and offering a compassionate ear can strengthen your bond. Empathy nurtures a connection that is based on mutual respect and understanding, making the relationship resilient and lasting.

Offer unconditional support

Being there for your friends during their times of need is

crucial. This means offering support without expecting anything in return. Whether it is a listening ear, a shoulder to cry on, or practical help, showing that you are there for them unconditionally reinforces the strength of your relationship. Your willingness to go out of your way to help them shows your commitment and loyalty.

Set aside ego

Deep relationships require humility and the ability to set aside your ego. This means prioritising the relationship over your pride and being willing to admit when you are wrong. It also involves forgiving mistakes and understanding that no one is perfect. By setting aside your ego, you create a space where honesty and vulnerability can thrive, which are essential components of a meaningful connection.

Have honest intentions

Honest intentions are fundamental to building trust and respect in any relationship. Be genuine in your interactions and avoid hidden agendas. When your intentions are clear and honest, it builds a solid foundation for a relationship that can withstand the test of time.

Investing in deep meaningful relationships is for life. Like any investment, it requires effort, but the returns are immeasurable. The support, love, and companionship we receive from these relationships are priceless. They remind us that we are not alone in this vast world, and they give us the courage to navigate through life's ups and downs.

Take a moment to reflect on your relationships. Are you investing in deep meaningful connections? Are there individuals in your life whom you can trust unconditionally? If not, it is never too late to start. Reach out to those who matter to you, invest time in nurturing these connections, and watch as they bloom into something beautiful. Remember, the truest measure of wealth lies not in our possessions or social-media popularity but in the quality of the relationships we cultivate.

Golden Rule:

Nurture your relationships, cherish them, and you will find that the richness they bring to your life far surpasses any material wealth.

#24 FIND YOUR PURPOSE AND FOLLOW IT

In a peaceful village nestled in the Hindu Kush mountains near the city of Kabul, in the early 18th century, there lived a respected Sufi by the name Hazrat Nasiruddin Shah Wali. He was renowned for his wisdom and serenity, and people from far and wide sought his guidance.

One day, a young, successful trader of carpets and silk named Ibrahim visited Hazrat Shah Wali. Ibrahim was troubled by a persistent sense of emptiness despite his material success. Ibrahim approached the Sufi and asked, "Hazrat, I have wealth, status, and comfort, yet I feel unfulfilled. What is the purpose of life?"

The Sufi smiled gently and handed Ibrahim a large, empty bowl. "Take this bowl and fill it with water from the river at the base of the mountain," he instructed.

Perplexed but obedient, Ibrahim made his way down the mountain to the river. As he began to fill the bowl, he noticed a small hole at the bottom, causing the water to leak out. Undeterred, he tried to fill it again and again, but the water kept seeping out. Frustrated and tired, he returned to the Sufi with the still-empty bowl.

"Hazrat, this bowl has a hole in it. No matter how much water I pour in, it will not stay full," Ibrahim exclaimed.

Hazrat Shah Wali nodded, his eyes twinkling. "Ah, Ibrahim, you have discovered the lesson. Your life, like this bowl, cannot be filled with external possessions alone. They will always leave you feeling empty because they are not your true purpose."

Ibrahim stared at the bowl, beginning to understand. "Then what is my true purpose, Hazrat?"

Hazrat Shah Wali replied, "Your true purpose is like the river itself, ever-flowing and nourishing all it touches. It is found in connection, compassion, and the pursuit of inner growth. When you live in harmony with your true purpose, your life, like the river, will be full and satisfying, no matter the material circumstances."

Ibrahim bowed deeply, grateful for the profound insight. From that day on, he sought to align his life with a deeper purpose, finding joy in meaningful connections, helping others, and attending to his own personal growth. The sense of emptiness faded, replaced by a lasting fulfilment that material success alone could never provide.

Purpose lies in creating value for the world using our own unique talents and abilities. **Finding meaning and purpose in life is the first step towards a journey of self-awareness and personal growth.** Each one of us arrives on this planet with a unique purpose, but as we grow up, social conditioning often obscures our true path. We fall into the trap of conforming to societal expectations, losing touch with our authentic selves and the purpose we were meant to fulfil.

At times, we may sense a deep hollowness and emptiness within, a longing for something more. Yet, we often drown out these feelings with work and distractions, avoiding the exploration of our true purpose. We convince ourselves that it is good enough to look after our responsibilities or simply take care of things in hand to live a successful and regret-free life.

It is undoubtedly important to work and do our duties. However, it is also important to take time for ourselves to ponder over life and its deeper meaning. We must connect with our purpose, as doing so gives us the opportunity to live a life of fulfilment that is free from regrets.

To discover our purpose, we must first identify our true passions – the activities that ignite a fire within us, make us lose track of time, and fill our hearts with joy. It is through these passions that we often stumble upon our purpose, by recognising how we can positively impact the lives of others through them. By aligning our passion with a greater cause or by working towards a meaningful goal, we fill our existence with deeper significance.

Discovering and pursuing our purpose is not a one-time destination, but an ongoing process. It requires introspection, self-reflection, and a willingness to explore new possibilities. Reflect on your values, beliefs, and strengths. Consider how you can utilise your unique skills and talents to make a positive difference in the world or in someone's life.

Embracing a sense of purpose provides us with direction and motivation. It gives us a reason to get up each day, knowing that our actions align with our deepest desires and values. Purpose fuels our drive, pushing us to overcome obstacles and embrace personal growth along the way.

However, it is important to note that finding your purpose does not necessarily mean a drastic career change or a complete life overhaul. Sometimes, it is about infusing purpose into your current circumstances, uncovering the meaning in the everyday moments. One of the top cardiologists from Gwalior, Dr Dushyant Deo, attended my workshop. He found his life's purpose through one of the sessions.

Dr Deo spends two to three hours every day practising medicine in a small village. He identifies children from zero to 18 years with congenital heart disease and those who need surgery to correct the problem. Till now he has performed 126 heart surgeries on children under government schemes where they do not have to bear any cost. Following his purpose gives him immense satisfaction. This is a classic example of how one can integrate his purpose of life with his work.

Remember, your purpose is not set in stone. It may evolve and change over time. Embrace the journey of self-discovery and allow yourself to explore different paths, always staying true to your authentic self.

As you embark on the quest to find your purpose, surround yourself with like-minded individuals who support and inspire you. Seek out mentors, engage in meaningful conversations, and learn from those who have discovered their own purpose.

Finding your purpose is not a solitary endeavour. It is a collective effort. Together, we can create a world where each individual lives a life aligned with their purpose, contributing their unique gifts and passions to make a positive impact in the world – a collective purpose.

Take the time to reflect, explore, and discover your purpose. Embrace the ongoing process of self-discovery and be open to the possibilities that lie ahead. Your purpose is waiting to be uncovered, guiding you towards a life of fulfilment, authenticity, and true meaning.

Golden Rule:

Discovering your purpose
isn't just about finding direction;
it's reclaiming your authenticity amidst
societal expectations, and living a life of
profound peace and contentment.

#25 | GET OUT OF YOUR COMFORT ZONE

There was once a family living on the outskirts of a remote village on a small plot of land. The only possession the family had was a cow. The life of the family was completely dependent on this animal. One day, a lone traveller stopped by the village. He was very hungry. Looking at his condition, the family shared the milk and cheese they had with him.

The traveller was extremely grateful for their generosity and wanted to return the favour and help the family, but did not know how.

He heard that there was a wise man in the village whom the villagers revered. He went to the wise man and told him about his concern. After hearing his problem, the wise man said, "Steal the cow."

"Steal it? How can that help them?" Unmoved, the wise man repeated, "Steal the cow." The traveller was nervous, but he went ahead and stole the cow that night, as advised by the wise man, and left for his destination.

A year later, the traveller happened to pass through the village again. He noticed that it had new shops and a thriving market.

He saw a new hotel that provided bed and breakfast for travellers.

The traveller entered the hotel. Behind the counter he found the eldest son of the same family. The man was standing tall, smiling and happy. The traveller greeted him and wanted to know how this transformation happened.

"We lost our cow. There was no milk. We had to go out and do something to be able to eat. We set up a small market, and it slowly grew. We also set up this hotel, which is now growing. Without the milk from our cow, we had to try new things. You can see the result."

Since the family was pushed out of their comfort zone, they had no option but to explore new possibilities of survival. The traveller now understood what the wise man intended. He was happy that he listened to him.

Most often we get so ensconced in our safe space that we are unaware of what we are capable of. Beyond the comfort zone lies our biggest success. When we venture outside of it, we give ourselves a chance to utilise our true potential. By challenging ourselves and pushing our boundaries, we discover new strengths, talents, and capabilities that we never knew existed. **If we remain within the confines of our comfort zone, we will never truly know what we are capable of achieving.**

Moreover, staying within our comfort zone means missing out on life's many good and exciting experiences. It is through exploring the unfamiliar and taking risks that we truly grow and evolve as individuals. Stepping out of our comfort zone can lead to unexpected opportunities, broadening our horizons, and providing invaluable lessons that shape our character.

Taking the first step is often the most important, as it helps overcome the inertia that holds us back. We must consciously and regularly step out of our comfort zones to break free from the shackles of familiarity and complacency. It is only by embracing discomfort and challenges that we can progress towards personal growth and success.

Many people fear taking risks because they fear failure or the unknown. However, it is precisely stepping into the unknown that can lead to new opportunities and experiences.

Embrace the unfamiliar, take calculated risks, and welcome the discomfort that comes with growth. It is in those moments of discomfort that one will find courage, resilience, and strength to overcome obstacles and achieve greatness.

Golden Rule:

Our biggest successes and most transformative experiences lie just beyond the boundaries of our comfort zone.

#26 | BE GOOD AT FORGIVING

There were two inseparable friends whose bond was famous in their village. They were always together, regardless of the season. One day, a minor misunderstanding escalated, and they stopped talking. One friend, consumed by anger, left the village, and started a new life in the city.

Years passed, and the friend in the city began to miss his old companion. He felt remorse for abandoning the friendship but was unsure how to seek forgiveness. Finally, he decided to take the first step and return to the village. On the train ride home, he confided in a fellow passenger that he had written a letter to his friend, asking for a sign of forgiveness. If his friend wanted him back, he was to tie a white cloth to the old tree at the centre of his farm.

As the train neared the village, the man was too nervous to look out the window. He asked his fellow passenger to look for him. When they rounded the bend, the passenger exclaimed, "Look! There is not only one cloth, there are hundreds! Every branch is covered!"

Forgiveness is crucial for emotional wellbeing and healthy relationships. Holding on to anger, resentment, guilt, and regret can prevent us from moving forward in life. By forgiving, we release this emotional baggage and find peace. The benefits of forgiveness include emotional healing, reduced stress and anxiety, improved relationships through trust and understanding, personal growth by fostering empathy and compassion, and better physical health by lowering blood pressure and reducing the risk of chronic illnesses.

Forgiveness is a process that requires effort and intention. Here are some tools and practices to help you let go of emotional baggage and embrace forgiveness:

Reflect on the situation

Take time to reflect on what happened. Understand the events from both perspectives. Acknowledge your feelings of hurt, anger, or betrayal, but also try to understand the other person's viewpoint.

Acknowledge your emotions

Allow yourself to feel the emotions associated with the situation. Suppressing feelings can make them bigger and aggravate them, but acknowledging them can be the first step toward healing.

Practise empathy

Put yourself in the other person's shoes. Empathy can help soften your heart and make forgiveness easier.

Communicate

If possible, talk to the person involved. Express your feelings calmly and listen to their side of the story. Open, honest communication can pave the way for understanding and reconciliation.

Write a letter

If direct communication is not possible or too difficult, write a letter expressing your feelings. You do not necessarily have to send it, but writing can be a therapeutic way to release pent-up emotions.

Let go of expectations

Understand that forgiveness does not mean condoning wrongdoing or expecting an apology. It is about freeing yourself from the negative emotions associated with the event.

Practise self-forgiveness

Forgive yourself for any role you may have played in the situation. Self-forgiveness is crucial for healing and moving forward.

Focus on the present and future

Shift your focus from the past to the present and future. Think about the positive outcomes of forgiveness and how it can improve your life and relationships.

Forgiveness is a powerful tool for emotional liberation and personal growth. It allows us to let go of the burdens of anger, resentment, guilt, and regret. By practising forgiveness, we can heal our hearts, mend our relationships, and find peace within ourselves. Remember, it is never too late to make the first move towards reconciliation.

Golden Rule:

Forgiveness is the key to emotional freedom and healthier relationships, allowing us to release anger and resentment for a more peaceful and fulfilling life.

#27 | BE EMPATHETIC

There was an elderly man seated on a bench in a busy mall. His eyes darted around, reflecting a sense of confusion and worry as he scanned the faces of people passing by. Ten minutes later, confused, he went and stood in the middle of the walkway, looking left and right repeatedly, clearly in distress. Many people were passing by and wondered what this man was up to but nobody really stopped to enquire. They just expressed their sympathy and went ahead.

After a while, a group of schoolchildren arrived there. When they saw the man, they went close to him and spoke gently, quickly understanding that he was lost and alone. One of them sprinted to the information desk while the others stayed behind, engaging the old man in conversation to soothe his nerves. Shortly after, a female security guard appeared, sent by mall authorities. She suggested the kids could leave, but they insisted on staying to comfort the old man.

An announcement echoed through the mall, and soon, a middle-aged couple arrived, visibly anxious. They explained that their elderly father was suffering from Alzheimer's disease, and they had been searching for him everywhere in the mall. Their relief was palpable. They expressed heartfelt gratitude to the mall staff and the schoolchildren for their help.

As the students walked away, the elderly man turned to the couple and remarked, "Those are some wonderful kids. You have done a great job raising them."

This story serves as a powerful reminder of the countless opportunities in daily life to extend empathy and kindness, much like these thoughtful schoolchildren did. Empathy is more than just understanding another person's feelings; it is the act of reaching out and making a positive difference in someone else's life.

In this instance, a group of schoolchildren exemplified empathy through their actions. They did not just notice the old man's distress, they took steps to alleviate it. Their willingness to stay by his side, despite the security guard's assurance that they could leave, demonstrated a commitment to kindness and understanding.

Empathy has the power to transform ordinary moments into extraordinary ones. It bridges the gap between strangers and creates a sense of community and care. The children's actions reassured the old man and provided comfort to the worried couple who had been searching for him.

In our fast-paced world, it is easy to overlook the struggles of those around us. However, by paying attention and extending a helping hand, we can create a ripple effect of compassion and support. Whether it is a simple smile, a kind word, or a more significant gesture like assisting someone in distress, every act of empathy contributes to a more connected and caring society.

Let this story inspire you to look for opportunities to practise empathy in your own life. Remember, the smallest actions can have the most significant impact. By choosing to care and understand, you can make a world of difference to someone in need.

Golden Rule:

Practise empathy and make a significant positive difference to someone in need.

#28 | LISTEN TO YOUR INNER VOICE

Rajat had a successful career as a financial consultant based in New Delhi. However, he felt a quiet yearning for something more fulfilling. This dissatisfaction experienced by Rajat from time to time reflected in his daily conduct and his relationships. Though his family valued stability and success, Rajat could not ignore his inner voice calling him to a different life. Seeking a brief escape, he joined a trekking group to the Himalayas, where the serene landscapes and towering peaks brought him a profound sense of peace. Sitting by a tranquil river, Rajat decided to leave New Delhi and live closer to nature.

Rajat faced scepticism from his family and friends, who worried about the uncertainty of his decision. Despite their concerns, he moved to a small village in Uttarakhand and started a homestay business for travellers and trekkers. The transition was challenging, but Rajat is a happy man today, as he finds immense satisfaction and joy in guiding treks, farming, and engaging with the local community. He radiates this peace and joy, making his family happy as well.

Deep inside us, there is a source of wisdom that goes beyond logic and reason. This wisdom knows every part of us, from our deepest thoughts to our biggest dreams. It is a quiet observer, a wise advisor, and a steady friend on our journey for meaning and happiness. This inner voice softly guides us, helping us navigate the twists and turns of life. It is like a compass inside us, helping us find our true direction.

Our inner voice speaks through our feelings, gently nudging us to make choices that match our true values and goals. It whispers softly, encouraging us to listen and trust its advice. When we quiet our busy minds and pay attention to this inner voice, we find clear insights that light up our way forward.

Listening to our inner voice takes patience, practice, and a willingness to be still. In the middle of life's chaos and distractions, finding moments of quiet helps us hear the gentle whispers of our soul. By making a conscious effort to connect with our inner self regularly, we can harness this power within and go through life with greater ease and purpose.

Connecting to your inner self involves delving into your subconscious mind. The key is to find practices that resonate with you and integrate them into your daily routine. One can tap into one's inner resources through meditation, journalling, visualisation, nature walks or through regular self-reflection.

Our inner voice is not merely a passive observer. It is a powerful force for transformation and growth. By listening to its whispers, we align ourselves with our true calling and highest potential. It gently nudges us toward choices and actions that resonate with our deepest values and aspirations, guiding us toward a life of meaning, fulfilment, and authenticity.

In a world filled with noise and distraction, our inner voice offers a sacred space where we can find solace, clarity, and guidance. By cultivating a practice of deep inner listening, we tap into the infinite reservoir of wisdom that resides within us, allowing its gentle whispers to illuminate our path and our journey.

Golden Rule:

Trust and follow your inner voice; it is the compass guiding you toward a life of authenticity, fulfilment, and true purpose.

#29 | MAKE A BUCKET LIST

One sunny afternoon, when a father and his young son were taking a leisurely walk through their small town, they passed an old cemetery. As they walked, the father noticed his son's curious gaze at the rows of graves. Pointing towards the cemetery, the father said with a thoughtful look on his face, "Son, here lies a great author, a painter, a musician, a scientist, a social worker, and a traveller."

The boy looked confused. "Really?" The father nodded. "Yes, but not in the way you think. These are people who had dreams, talents, and possibilities. Many of them had the potential. But for various reasons, they never fulfilled those dreams."

The boy asked, trying to understand. "Why didn't they do those things, Dad?"

The father sighed. "There are many reasons, son. But most importantly they were probably not clear about what they really wished to achieve. A few were too afraid to take risks, or were held back by circumstances or did not believe in themselves. Sometimes, life just got in the way. It is a waste of talent and possibilities that could never be completed or fulfilled in their lifetime."

The boy looked back at the graves, "I don't want to end up like that, Dad. I want to do all the things I dream of."

The father smiled, and said, "You can, son. But first make a list of things you want to do. That will bring clarity in your mind about your goals. Always listen to your inner voice and follow your dreams. And then, do not let fear or doubt hold you back. Life is short, and you must make the most of the moments you have, so that when your time comes, you can say you have no regrets."

We all have our dreams, aspirations, things to do and achieve, before we kick the bucket. But we are mostly unaware. This is because, most often, our list is governed by what people tell us to do or achieve or societal expectations or norms. We must first be clear about what we want to do or achieve. And it is imperative to create a list of those things.

I feel blessed to have shared my father's final years with him. In our earlier years, we rarely spoke much, but everything changed as he grew older. When he began to lose his mobility, I started to spend more time by his side, engaging in deep conversations. We talked about many things, but the moments that stood out were when he opened up about his life – his dreams, his unfulfilled aspirations, and the things he wished he had done. I could sense his regrets in those quiet confessions, the weight of missed opportunities hanging in the air. Each conversation was a window into his soul, revealing the man behind the father I thought I knew.

That is when I realised the importance of making a bucket list. A bucket list is a compilation of experiences and accomplishments you want to achieve before you leave this world. This is a powerful exercise in self-reflection and goal-setting. It brings clarity to your aspirations, ignites a sense of urgency, and reminds you of the importance of your own life and dreams.

The act of making a bucket list also instils a sense of urgency. My friend Meghna always wanted to run a marathon but kept postponing it. When she finally added it to her bucket list, she felt a renewed sense of determination. She began training, completed her first marathon within a year, and experienced a profound sense of achievement. The bucket list served as a reminder that life is fleeting, and time waits for no one. It motivated her to seize the present moment and avoid falling into the trap of procrastination.

A bucket list prompts us to take stock of our resources and the time we have available to achieve our dreams. For instance, if your bucket list includes learning to play the guitar, you might assess your current schedule and decide to take lessons twice a week. By evaluating the feasibility of your goals, you can better allocate your time, energy, and resources to bring them to fruition.

Take a paper and pen and write down the things you want to do during this lifetime. List things you can measure, so that you can tick them off as you go along. Avoid writing vague things such as, "I want to help as many people as possible," or "I want to spread happiness," because they are not tangible goals. Creating a bucket list is not an overnight process. You may want to revisit and edit the list from time to time because you evolve with time and get clarity about the things you really want to achieve.

Write down your dreams, big and small, without limitations or judgement. Let your imagination run wild and envision a life lived to the fullest. Whether it is skydiving, starting a charity, or learning a new language, make the commitment to yourself to pursue your dreams with passion and determination. Your bucket list is not just a list of desires; it is a declaration of your intention to the universe to live a life that reflects your deepest aspirations.

Golden Rule:

Listen to your inner voice and create a bucket list that reflects your true aspirations. It is a roadmap to living a life aligned with your dreams.

#30 | NEVER EVER GIVE UP

Kieran Behan was born on April 19, 1989, in London to Irish parents. Behan was passionate about gymnastics as a child, but his journey took a dramatic turn when he was just 10 years old.

He was diagnosed with a benign tumour in his left thigh. The surgery to remove the tumour went tragically wrong, resulting in severe nerve damage. This left him in a wheelchair, unable to walk. Doctors informed him that he might never walk again, let alone return to gymnastics.

Despite this terrible prognosis, Behan was determined to overcome his disability. He spent more than a year in intensive rehabilitation, enduring unbearable pain and setbacks. His unwavering determination saw him gradually regain the ability to walk, and he eventually returned to gymnastics training. However, his battle was far from over.

Shortly after his return, Behan suffered a catastrophic accident in the gym. He fell from the high bar and hit his head, causing a traumatic brain injury. The injury resulted in serious complications, including frequent blackouts and memory loss. He was forced to take significant time off from school and gymnastics, and once again, doctors doubted his ability to continue in the sport.

Behan's resolve was tested again, but he refused to give up. He went through another gruelling recovery process, learning to cope with his injuries and rebuilding his strength and skills. His journey back to competitive gymnastics was slow and fraught with difficulties, but his resolve never wavered.

Kieran Behan's perseverance finally paid off. In 2011, he made history by becoming the first Irish gymnast to win a World Cup medal. He earned a gold medal on the floor exercise at the FIG World Challenge Cup in Doha. This achievement marked a significant milestone in his career, proving that he could compete with the best in the world.

In 2012, Behan's dream of competing in the Olympics became a reality. He qualified for the 2012 London Olympics, becoming only the second gymnast from Ireland to do so. Although he did not win any medal, his participation alone was a remarkable achievement and an inspiration to many.

Kieran Behan's story is an extraordinary tale of overcoming adversity and achieving greatness against all odds. His journey was filled with significant challenges that would have deterred most people. It is not just about his achievements in gymnastics but also about his extraordinary resilience and spirit.

Behan's journey from a wheelchair to the Olympic stage, and hundreds of similar other stories of people who would not quit, serve as a powerful reminder of what can be achieved with perseverance and a positive mindset.

Persistence is the key to overcoming adversity and achieving success. Life's journey is filled with obstacles, setbacks, and unexpected turns, but it is our determination and resolve that define our ability to rise above these challenges. Giving up may seem like the easier path in moments of difficulty, but it robs us of the opportunity to learn, grow, and ultimately triumph. Each setback is a chance to build strength, gain wisdom, and develop a deeper understanding of ourselves and our capabilities. If we have an unwavering commitment to our goals and dreams, even in the face of hardship, we can harness the power of perseverance, turning obstacles into stepping stones. Remember, true success is not measured by the absence of challenges, but by the courage to keep moving forward, no matter how tough the journey gets.

During hard times, even strong people tend to give up. But if you do not quit and keep moving forward, you will be able to overcome difficulties. And the hard times will pass.

'Never ever giving up' means having the strength to endure tough times and bounce back from life's challenges. It does not mean you will not feel stress, sadness, or pain along the way. Resilience isn't just about being tough; it is about facing emotional struggles head-on and finding a way to overcome them. Keep pushing forward.

Golden Rule:

No matter the obstacles,
never give up on your dreams;
resilience and determination can overcome any challenge.

#31 | YOU ARE BIGGER THAN YOUR PROBLEMS

In a tranquil village, there lived an old master who was revered for his wisdom. People from near and far came to seek his guidance, pouring out their troubles and seeking solace in his words. Among his many followers was a young man known for his constant complaints about life's hardships. The master, patient and kind, had grown weary of the young man's incessant whining.

One morning, the master decided it was time to teach his follower a profound lesson. So, he sent the young man to fetch some salt. When the follower returned, the master instructed him to mix a handful of salt in a glass of water and drink it.

"How does it taste?" the master asked.

"Bitter," the young man replied with a frown.

The master chuckled softly. "Now, take the same handful of salt and put it in the lake," he said.

The two walked in silence to a nearby lake. The young man obediently sprinkled a handful of salt into the water and stirred it. The master then told him to drink from the lake.

As the young man tasted the water, the master asked, "How does it taste?"

"Fresh," the young man remarked.

"Do you taste the salt?" inquired the master.

"No," came the young man's response.

The master sat down beside the young man and explained gently, "The pain of life is like salt – no more, no less. The amount of pain in life remains constant, like the handful of salt. However, the bitterness we taste depends on the container we put it in. When you are in pain, the only thing you can do is to expand your life and enlarge your sense of things. Stop being a glass. Become a lake."

Life is full of challenges, and it is easy to become consumed by them. The more we focus on our problems, the more overwhelming and impossible they appear. This is why a shift in perspective is essential. Instead of being fixated on the problem, we must focus on solutions and adopt a solution-oriented mindset.

One of the first steps towards this shift is to stop complaining. Constant complaining rewires our brain in such a way that we can see only problems in every aspect of life. This reinforces a negative mindset, and we stop looking at the positives. By breaking this habit, we open ourselves up to new possibilities and opportunities.

To effectively address a problem, we must take a step back and seek to understand its root cause. This clarity allows us to approach the situation with insight and objectivity.

Reflecting on past experiences is also important. Identify what has worked in similar situations and adapt those lessons to the current problem. Sometimes, the solution lies in the lessons we have already learnt.

When we examine our lives from a wider perspective, we often realise that our problems are relatively small in the grand scheme of things. And every problem has a solution, even if it is not immediately apparent.

Always remember, you are bigger than your problems. Trust in your abilities, have unwavering faith, and hold the perspective that no challenge can overpower your resilience and inner strength. With this mindset, you will navigate life's hurdles with grace and emerge stronger on the other side.

Golden Rule:

Shift your focus from problems to solutions, adopting a positive mindset to navigate life's challenges with flexibility and strength.

#32 HUMILITY IS A SIGN OF GREATNESS

The River was very proud of the tremendous flow of its water. The River felt, "I am so powerful that I can wash away everything with me – the mountains, houses, trees, animals, humans, everything."

One day, the River proudly asked the Ocean, "Tell me, what should I bring for you? Houses, animals, humans, trees, whatever you want, I can uproot it and bring with me."

The Ocean understood that the River had become egoistic. So, it said to the River, "If you want to bring something for me, uproot some Grass and bring it."

The River, filled with ego and arrogance, said, "Is that all? I'll bring it right away."

While passing through the field, the River exerted its full force on the Grass, but the Grass did not get uprooted. The River tried several times, but failed.

Eventually the River gave up and reached the Ocean and said, "I can uproot trees, houses, mountains, even animals. But whenever I apply force to uproot the Grass, it just bends down and I have to pass from above, empty-handed."

The Ocean listened carefully to the River and said, "Those who are hard and rigid like mountains and trees, are easily uprooted. But the one who has learnt the humility of Grass cannot be disturbed even by the fiercest of winds or violent storms. Grass does not resist your force. Instead, it bends and sways with you, yielding to your power. Its strength lies in its flexibility and ability to adapt. By remaining humble it can endure where even the mightiest can fall."

The River realised the deep wisdom in the Ocean's words. From that day on, the River treated everyone with gentle respect, understanding that their humble nature held an immense strength.

Humility is one of the most profound virtues a person can possess. It is the quality that grounds greatness, nurtures growth, and creates a harmonious balance in life. Far from being a sign of weakness, humility is a powerful force that shapes character, enhances relationships, and guides individuals towards true wisdom and strength.

Humility is the recognition and acceptance of one's limitations, combined with the appreciation of the value and contributions of others. It is the understanding that no matter how much one knows, there is always more to learn. Humility allows individuals to remain open-minded, seek knowledge, and accept constructive criticism.

History is replete with examples of great individuals whose humility defined their legacy. Mahatma Gandhi, despite leading a massive movement for India's independence, lived a life of simplicity and self-discipline. His humility and willingness to listen to others garnered immense respect and allowed him to lead effectively without resorting to force. Similarly, former President of India and a top aerospace scientist Dr APJ Abdul Kalam, whom I was fortunate to have personally interacted with, was an epitome of humility himself. During my meeting with him, when I presented him my books, he said, "Now what can I give you from my side?" Rising from his chair, he personally picked a couple of his books from the shelf, signed them and gave them to me with his blessings.

In leadership, humility is a cornerstone of effective management and influence. A humble leader values the inputs of their team, encourages an inclusive environment, and leads by example. They do not seek to dominate but to empower others, recognising that collective success is far more sustainable than individual accolades.

Humility in leadership also means being accountable for one's actions. A humble leader admits when they are wrong, learns from their mistakes, and takes steps to rectify them. This transparency builds trust and loyalty among team members, creating a strong, cohesive unit.

One of the most intriguing aspects of humility is its relationship with confidence. True humility does not mean undervaluing oneself or being timid. Instead, it is a balanced state where one has a realistic understanding of one's strengths and weaknesses. Humility and confidence can coexist, where confidence stems from a deep-seated knowledge of one's abilities, while humility ensures that this confidence does not turn into arrogance.

Humility is not confined to grand historical figures or leaders; it is a virtue that can be cultivated in everyday life. It can be practised through small acts of kindness, gratitude, and respect for others. Listening attentively, acknowledging the efforts of others, and being open to different perspectives are simple yet powerful ways to embody humility.

In personal relationships, humility creates deeper connections and understanding. It allows individuals to communicate openly, resolve conflicts amicably, and build a foundation of mutual respect and trust. **A humble person is more likely to empathise with others, creating a supportive and nurturing environment.**

The benefits of humility extend beyond personal growth and better relationships. Research has shown that humble individuals are generally happier and more content. They experience less stress and anxiety, as they do not constantly seek validation or compete with others. Humility also enhances mental strength, as humble individuals are more adaptable and open to change.

Moreover, humility cultivates a sense of gratitude. When one acknowledges their limitations and appreciates the contributions of others, they are more likely to feel grateful for the support and opportunities they receive. This gratitude, in turn, leads to a more positive outlook on life and greater overall wellbeing.

Cultivating humility requires conscious effort and self-reflection. Here are some steps to develop this vital virtue:

Self-awareness: Reflect on your strengths and weaknesses. Acknowledge your limitations and areas for improvement.

Gratitude: Practise gratitude by regularly acknowledging the contributions and support of others.

Listening: Develop active listening skills. Pay attention to others' perspectives without interrupting or dismissing them.

Open-mindedness: Be open to feedback and willing to learn from others, regardless of their status or background.

Service: Engage in acts of service. Helping others brings in a sense of humility and reinforces the value of community and collaboration.

Humility is a great virtue that lies at the heart of true greatness. It is the foundation upon which character, wisdom, and strength are built. In a world that often values self-promotion and competition, humility stands as a beacon of true excellence, guiding us towards a more harmonious and satisfying life.

Golden Rule:

Humility paves the way to true greatness.

#33 | DO NOT TAKE LIFE TOO SERIOUSLY

One day, at a prestigious company in London, a very serious and hardworking executive named Mr Langley was working late into the night. He was known for his no-nonsense attitude and his dedication to his job. The cleaning staff had already started their rounds, and among them was Maria, an older lady with a great sense of humour.

As Maria entered Mr Langley's office to clean, she noticed how intensely focused he was on his computer screen. Trying to lighten the mood, she said, "You know, Mr Langley, all work and no play makes Jack a dull boy."

Mr Langley, barely looking up, replied, "Maria, if I don't finish this report, the board meeting tomorrow will be a disaster. There's no time for play." Maria, undeterred, glanced around the room and spotted a small, decorative box on his desk. Without a word, she opened it and pulled out a clown nose. With a mischievous grin, she put it on and stood in front of him, crossing her eyes and making funny faces. Mr Langley couldn't help but chuckle at the sight. "Maria, what on earth are you doing?" he asked, unable to suppress a smile.

"Sometimes, Mr Langley, you just need to put on a clown nose and laugh at the absurdity of it all," she replied, still making funny faces. "Life's too short to be serious all the time."

Mr Langley paused, leaned back in his chair, and took a deep breath. "You know what, Maria? You're right." He took the clown nose from her and put it on himself, making a ridiculous face that sent Maria into fits of laughter.

For the first time in a long while, Mr Langley laughed too. And in that moment, he realised that a little laughter could go a long way in making life's burdens feel a bit lighter.

The next day, Mr Langley went into the board meeting with a new perspective. He was prepared, and he had also learnt the value of not taking life too seriously. And on his desk, the clown nose stayed as a reminder to always find a moment to laugh.

Life has a way of throwing curveballs when we least expect them. At times, the challenges we face can seem impossible, and the world can appear overwhelmingly dark and hopeless. However, there is a golden rule that can help us navigate even the most difficult times with grace and resilience – do not take life too seriously. **By embracing humour and finding the absurdity in our struggles, we can lighten our burdens and rediscover the joy of living.**

Laughter is a universal language, a natural antidote to stress and a powerful tool for maintaining perspective. When we laugh, we release natural feel-good chemicals, which can help reduce pain and improve our mood. Laughter also improves social connections, strengthens relationships, and enhances our ability to cope with adversity. Humour has the ability to dismantle even the most formidable barriers, offering us a fresh outlook on our circumstances.

Life is inherently unpredictable. When we recognise and accept this, we can start to see the humour in our daily experiences. This does not mean we should ignore our problems or avoid dealing with serious issues; rather, it means approaching life with a sense of playfulness and an open heart.

Kabir, a middle-aged man, lost his job due to company downsizing. Initially, Kabir was devastated. He felt a profound sense of loss and anxiety about his future. One day, as he was moping around the house, he tripped over his dog's chew toy and landed face-first in a pile of laundry. As he lay there, tangled in socks and underwear, he could not help but laugh at the ridiculousness of the situation. That moment of laughter was a turning point for Kabir. It did not solve his problems, but it gave him the emotional release he needed to start looking at his situation with a new perspective. He began to explore new career opportunities with a lighter heart, eventually finding a job that he loved.

To cultivate a habit of not taking life too seriously, we can practise finding humour in our daily experiences. Here are some strategies to help you embrace this mindset.

Laugh at yourself

Do not be afraid to laugh at your own mistakes and quirks. Making light of your eccentricities can be extremely liberating and can help you connect with others on a deeper level.

Surround yourself with laughter

Spend time with people who make you laugh. Whether it is watching a funny movie, reading a humorous book, or listening to a comedy podcast, make laughter a regular part of your life.

Reframe challenges

When faced with a difficult situation, ask yourself, "What's funny about this?" or "How will I laugh about this in the future?" This shift in perspective can help you navigate challenges with a lighter heart.

Be playful

Allow yourself to be silly and playful, regardless of your age. Engage in activities that make you feel like a child again, whether it is playing a game, dancing, or simply being goofy with friends and family.

Change your perspective

One of the greatest gifts of humour is its ability to provide a different perspective. When we do not take life too seriously, we can step back and see the bigger picture. We realise that our problems, while significant, are just a small part of our overall journey. This broader perspective can help us remain resilient and hopeful, even in the face of adversity.

Julia always dreamed of travelling the world. After years of saving, she finally booked a trip to Europe. However, her plans were derailed when her luggage was lost, and she missed a connecting flight. Initially, Julia was frustrated and disheartened. But as she sat in the airport, she overheard a child laughing hysterically at a silly joke. The sound of that laughter reminded her of the joy and spontaneity she had sought in her travels. She decided to embrace the chaos, treating her unexpected detour as an adventure. Julia ended up making new friends and discovering hidden gems that were not on her original itinerary, turning what could have been a disaster into one of the most memorable experiences of her life.

In the grand scheme of things, life is a fleeting and unpredictable journey. By choosing not to take it too seriously, we can navigate its ups and downs with a sense of humour and lightness. Laughter is not a cure-all, but it is a powerful tool that can help us maintain our sanity, make connections, and find joy even in the darkest times.

Golden Rule:

When life throws you a curveball, take a deep breath, find the humour in the situation, and remember that it is all part of the beautiful, absurd adventure of being alive.

#34 | BE AUTHENTIC

Adrian was a famous movie star, adored by fans worldwide, living a life of glamour and luxury. His public image was one of charm and charisma, but behind the scenes, his assistant Zoya knew the truth. Zoya saw firsthand how badly Adrian treated women, leaving them hurt and heartbroken. She grew weary of his duplicity and eventually quit her job to pursue her dreams. Adrian, accustomed to having everything go his way, was shocked by Zoya's departure. He realised that she had been more than just an assistant. Desperate to reconcile, he went to her house, only to find her younger sister Clair at home.

Clair was a celebrated writer, modest and humble despite her numerous awards. She was authentic in a way Adrian had never encountered. Intrigued and attracted, Adrian found himself drawn to her genuine nature. They began meeting regularly, and Clair's lack of interest in his fame and her grounded personality captivated him. Slowly, Adrian started to fall in love with Clair, feeling more authentic and unmasked in her presence than he ever had before.

When Zoya learnt about this relationship, she feared Clair would end up like the other women in Adrian's life. Determined to protect her sister, Zoya intervened, not allowing them to meet. Adrian realised that for the first time in his life, he wanted to be his true self, without pretence. He understood the importance of authenticity and how living a life of falsehood had cost him genuine connections.

Adrian approached Zoya and explained how Clair had changed him. He assured her that his love for Clair was real and that he had no intentions of hurting her. Moved by his honesty and seeing the change in him, Zoya reluctantly allowed them to see each other again.

Clair and Adrian's relationship flourished, built on mutual respect and genuine affection. Adrian, shedding his masks, found true happiness and contentment in being authentic.

In the journey of life, there is a golden rule that shines brighter than most – authenticity. Being authentic means embracing who you are at your core, without pretension or disguise. It is a principle that encourages us to live truthfully and transparently, to align our actions with our values, and to present ourselves genuinely to the world.

Authenticity is the state of being true to one's own personality, spirit, and character despite external pressures. It is about being real and honest, not only with others but with ourselves. In a world that often rewards conformity and superficiality, staying true to oneself can be a radical act of courage and self-respect.

We often wear masks to fit in, to be liked, or to meet societal expectations. These masks can take many forms, such as pretending to enjoy activities we dislike, agreeing with opinions we oppose, or even suppressing our dreams and desires. While these masks might help us navigate social situations more smoothly, they ultimately prevent us from connecting deeply with others and living fulfilling lives.

When we are true to ourselves, we attract people who appreciate us for who we are, not for who we pretend to be. These relationships are more satisfying and lasting because they are built on a foundation of trust and honesty.

Cultivating authenticity is an ongoing process that involves self-awareness, courage, and a commitment to personal growth. Here are some steps to help you embrace your authentic self.

Know yourself

Spend time reflecting on your values, passions, and strengths. journalling, meditation, and self-assessment can aid in this discovery. Understand what makes you unique and what you truly want from life.

Accept yourself

Embrace your imperfections and vulnerabilities. Recognise that nobody is perfect, and it is our oddities and flaws that make us human. Accepting ourselves unconditionally is a crucial step toward living authentically.

Express yourself

Share your thoughts, feelings, and opinions openly and honestly. Practise assertive communication and set boundaries to protect your integrity. Remember, it is okay to disagree and to have different perspectives.

Align your actions

Ensure that your actions reflect your values and beliefs. Make decisions that are true to who you are, even if they are not popular or easy. This alignment creates a sense of coherence and genuineness in your life.

Embrace change

Authenticity does not mean being static. As you grow and evolve, your authentic self may change. Be open to new experiences and perspectives, and allow yourself to transform.

The impact of authenticity extends beyond personal fulfilment. It can inspire others to be genuine and courageous in their own lives. When we live authentically, we may become role models for others, to show that it is possible to navigate life with honesty and integrity.

The journey to authenticity is a lifelong process, but it is a journey worth taking. Always be true, be real, be you.

Golden Rule:

***Live a life of authenticity.
It is liberating, and a key to
genuine relationships and lasting happiness.***

#35 | BE A GOOD LISTENER

This remarkable story left a lasting impression on me.

One day, Johnny decided to create something new, special, and amazing. He worked tirelessly and made something he was incredibly proud of. But then, out of nowhere, a strong wind came and destroyed everything he had built. Johnny was devastated, utterly heartbroken.

First to notice was the neighbour, who expressed his sympathy and offered to talk about it. But Johnny was not in the mood for talking, so the neighbour left. Next, a friend came by and suggested shouting about it to release the anger, but Johnny did not feel like shouting either, so the friend left too.

An older relative visited and offered to help rebuild – suggesting that she remembered exactly how things were – and recreate it. But Johnny did not want to remember, so the relative also left. One by one, others came with their own suggestions: laughing it off, pretending it never happened, throwing everything away, or even taking out the frustration on someone else. But Johnny was not interested in any of these ideas, so they all left, one by one.

Eventually, Johnny was alone in the room in silence. He did not notice when a friend, Giny, whom he had never really acknowledged, sat down next to him. Giny did not say anything, just sat there, offering silent companionship. Johnny felt her presence and warmth, and after a while, he began to talk. Giny listened with understanding as Johnny shared his sorrow, his anger, his memories, and even his laughter. She listened to Johnny's desire to hide, to discard everything, to seek revenge. Giny stayed through it all, without judging, criticising, or offering advice.

Finally, when Johnny was ready, he talked about his plan to build again. "I can't wait," he said. "It's going to be amazing." Giny listened, unwavering, just nodding once in a while.

When going through a challenging time, listening acts as a powerful healing tool. Most often, you come up with your own solutions, as you know your situation the best. What you need is just a listening ear and someone to empathise with you.

Listening with empathy is about stepping into the other person's shoes and seeing the world from their perspective. It requires suspending judgement and focusing entirely on understanding their feelings and experiences. When someone feels heard and understood, it can significantly impact their emotional wellbeing.

In the noise of modern life, genuine listening has become a rare skill. We often hear without truly listening, with an inbuilt urge to respond and reply, missing the opportunity to connect deeply with those around us. The art of listening goes beyond simply absorbing words. It involves understanding the emotions, intentions, and unspoken messages behind those words. The interesting fact is that only 20 percent of our communication is verbal, whereas 80 percent is non-verbal.

Here are a few practical steps to improve listening:

Be present: Set aside distractions and focus entirely on the speaker. Practise mindfulness techniques to help you stay in the moment.

Show interest: Use body language to demonstrate your engagement. Lean forward slightly, maintain eye contact, and nod encouragingly.

Avoid interrupting: Let the speaker finish their thoughts before you respond. Resist the urge to interject with your own stories or solutions.

Reflect and clarify: Paraphrase what the speaker has said to ensure you understand correctly. Ask further questions to clarify, if needed.

Practise empathy: Try to understand the speaker's emotions and perspectives. Validate their feelings without offering unsolicited advice.

Embrace silence: Allow pauses in the conversation. Silence can encourage deeper reflection and sharing.

Listening is a profound act of love and respect. Being a good listener bridges gaps, heals wounds, and nurtures connections. By honing the art of listening, we not only enrich our own lives but also contribute positively to the lives of those around us. In a world that often feels disconnected, the simple act of truly listening can be a powerful force for change.

Golden Rule:

Being good in listening, with empathy and without judgement, results in healing and deeper connections.

#36 | NEVER BREAK ANYONE'S TRUST

I came across an inspiring anecdote about a father's unwavering determination to rescue his son from the rubble of an earthquake. While the author is unknown, the message of love, trust, and perseverance deeply resonated with me.

In the country of Armenia, in 1988, Erik and Milena sent their young son Aram off to school. Before leaving, Erik squatted before his son, looked him in the eye, and said, "Have a good day at school, and remember, no matter what, I'll always be there for you." They hugged and the boy ran off to school.

Hours later, a powerful earthquake rocked the area. In the midst of the pandemonium, Erik and Milena tried to discover what happened to their son but they couldn't get any information. The radio announced that there were thousands of casualties.

Erik then grabbed his coat and headed for the school. When he reached the area, what he saw brought tears to his eyes. Aram's school was a pile of debris. Other parents were standing around crying.

Erik found the place where Aram's classroom used to be and began pulling a broken beam off the pile of rubble. He then grabbed a rock and put it to the side, and then grabbed another one.

One of the parents looking on asked, "What are you doing?"

"Digging for my son," Erik answered.

The man then said, "You are just going to make things worse. The building is unstable," and tried to pull Erik away from his work.

Erik just kept working. As time passed on, one by one, the other parents left. Then a worker tried to pull Erik away from the rubble. Erik looked at him and said, "Won't you help me?" The worker left as well. All through the night and into the next day, Erik continued digging. Parents placed flowers and pictures of their children on the ruins, but Erik just kept working.

He picked up a beam and pushed it out of the way when he heard a faint cry. "Help! Help!" Erik listened but did not hear anything again. Then he heard a muffled voice, "Papa?"

Erik began to dig furiously. Finally, he could see his son. "Come on out, son!" he said with relief.

"No," Aram said. "Let the other kids come out first because I know you'll get me." Child after child emerged until, finally, little Aram appeared. Erik took him in his arms and Aram said, "I told the other kids not to worry because you told me that you'd always be there for me."

Fourteen children were saved that day because one father kept his word.

Trust is one of the four pillars upon which all meaningful relationships are built, other pillars being love, commitment, and communication. It is a delicate bond, easily fractured yet incredibly resilient when nurtured with care and respect. Building trust is a basic requirement to all healthy relationships, whether personal or professional.

However, trust is not built overnight. Trust is earned through consistent effort, honesty, and reliability over a period of time. When people know that they can count on you, follow through on commitments, and be transparent, they feel secure in their interactions with you. This security nurtures deeper connections, open communication, and mutual respect. Being dependable in small, everyday situations, as well as in significant matters, reinforces the trust others place in you. Over time, this creates a strong bond that can withstand challenges and misunderstandings.

There is another interesting story on trust.

One cold night, a billionaire encountered an old, poor man outside. Concerned, he asked, "Aren't you cold without a coat?" The old man replied, "I don't have one, but I've grown used to it." The billionaire said, "Wait here. I'll go inside and bring you a coat." The poor man smiled, grateful, and agreed to wait.

The billionaire went inside but got distracted and forgot about the poor man. The next morning, he remembered and rushed outside to find the old man, but it was too late. The poor man had succumbed to the cold. When he had no warm clothes, he had the strength to endure because he was used to it. The billionaire's promise gave him false expectations thate took away his resilience.

Do not promise anything if you can't keep your promise. It might not mean anything to you, but it could mean everything to someone else.

Breaking someone's trust can have profound and lasting effects. Once it is broken, it can take ages to repair the dent that is created and bring it back to the same level. It can lead to feelings of betrayal and hurt. It weakens the foundation of any relationship, causing people to become guarded and hesitant to open up. The damage can affect not only the people directly involved but also those around them. To break someone's trust is to shatter not only their confidence in you but also the very essence of the relationship itself. It is betrayal that echoes long after the deed is done, leaving behind scars that may never fully heal.

Therefore, it is crucial to handle trust with care and integrity. If you make a mistake, acknowledge it, offering a sincere apology, and make changes that can help in the healing process.

Always remember – never break anyone's trust. It is a golden rule of life that upholds the sanctity of human connection and the integrity of your character.

Golden Rule:

Building trust takes sincere efforts and time. Never ever break anyone's trust.

#37 DO THINGS YOU LOVED DOING AS A CHILD

I came to Mumbai immediately after my graduation, and started my career in the steel industry as a graduate engineer trainee. Many years later, when I visited my birthplace Gwalior, the city had significantly changed. But the places where I stayed and grew up still had many childhood memories attached to them.

The sunlit afternoons of my childhood were filled with boundless joy and adventure, where every day felt like an endless summer vacation. Memories of the thrill of racing with my friends through the fields – the sound of our laughter echoing as we played among the trees – rushed back to me. The smell of fresh-cut grass and the taste of homemade ice-cream, shared in secret forts built from blankets, sticks, and furniture, remain vivid. I remembered the games I used to play with friends, such as I spy (hide and seek), *sataulia* (seven stones), *langdi*, chain, *kanche*, *gilli-danda*, statue, and *galli-cricket*, or swinging as high as we could imagining we could touch the sky, or simply running around without any specific reason. The joy these small unimportant things used to give was immeasurable. Even now, when I remember those days, I am filled with happiness and thrill.

As time passes, many childhood memories start to fade. And that is because our mind needs to make space for new experiences. But we often turn to photos and other things that remind us of the feelings we experienced as a child. These feelings and emotions of childhood help us to reconnect with our childhood persona, which was completely carefree, happy, and free from stresses and anxieties.

Engaging in activities we loved as children holds the power to ignite true happiness within us. It transports us back in time when we were unburdened by stress, anxieties, and emotional baggage. In childhood, every moment was filled with joy, unconditional love, and acceptance. There were no barriers or conditions hindering our pursuit of happiness. You must have noticed how playing with small children helps us connect with the child within us too.

As adults, we often carry a heavy load of negative emotions with us. These emotions act as barriers, preventing us from fully embracing the present moment and experiencing pure joy. The weight of responsibilities and the pressures of adulthood can sometimes leave us feeling overwhelmed and detached from the innocence and boundless happiness we once knew.

However, when we engage in activities that once brought us joy as children, a remarkable transformation occurs. We reconnect with the carefree spirit within us, allowing us to experience a sense of freedom and boundless energy. It is as if we are reclaiming a part of ourselves that was temporarily lost amidst the trials and tribulations of growing up.

The beauty of engaging in childhood activities lies in their ability to release us from the shackles of everyday life. They remind us to approach life with cheerfulness that is often forgotten in the busyness of adulthood. Whether it is playing a sport, drawing, dancing, or simply running through a field, these activities rekindle a childlike sense of wonder and enthusiasm.

By realigning ourselves with the activities we once loved, we create space for happiness and playfulness in our lives. We tap into the wellspring of joy that resides within us, and suddenly, the weight of our responsibilities feels a little lighter. These moments of childlike bliss remind us that life is not solely about duties and obligations but also about embracing the simple pleasures that bring us true happiness.

Take a moment to reflect on the activities that brought you joy as a child. What made your heart sing? What made you feel alive and carefree? Revisit these activities, no matter how small or seemingly insignificant. Allow yourself to fully immerse in the experience, relishing the freedom and pure joy they bring.

In doing so, you will discover that the child within you is still alive, waiting to be awakened.

Remember, engaging in the activities you loved as a child is not a regression but an act of self-care and self-discovery. It is an acknowledgment that amidst the complexities of adult life, there is still room for childlike joy and innocence. So, make time for the activities that once made your heart soar and watch as the magic of childhood unfolds before you once again.

Golden Rule:

Reconnect with the joy of your inner child by engaging in activities that once brought you happiness.

#38 HANDLE CRITICISM WITH GRACE

In a small village in Arabia, in the 1800s, there lived a master calligrapher named Amir al-Farisi. Amir was renowned far and wide not only for his beautiful work but also for his humility.

One day, two young trainees came to Amir al-Farisi, seeking to learn the art of calligraphy. One was the egotistic and brash Qasim and the other was the shy and subdued Nadia. While Qasim was eager to prove himself, Nadia, although talented, was always silent.

Soon, Qasim completed a piece and presented it to Amir for feedback. Instead of offering gentle advice, Amir al-Farisi looked at the piece and said, "Wallah, this is terrible. Your strokes are untidy, and your composition is weak." Nadia had just started, but could not finish. Amir gently told her to finish whatever she could, and motivated her saying that she could become the best. Qasim's face reddened with anger and embarrassment.

Determined to prove his worth, Qasim spent the next week practising diligently, only to receive the same harsh criticism. Nadia, on the other hand, was making slow but good progress due to the continued praise and motivation by Amir. This cycle repeated for several months, until one day Qasim's patience snapped. "Why do you keep criticising my work so harshly? On the other hand, you are always praising Nadia, although she is not as talented as me. Are you trying to make me give up?" he demanded.

Amir al-Farisi smiled gently and replied, "I criticise you harshly because I see potential in you. You have the talent, but you lack the patience to become perfect. Every time you face my criticism and return with better work, you grow. Handling criticism with grace is as much a part of your training as mastering the brush. On the other hand, Nadia is a person with low self-esteem. She needs praise and motivation because she does not know that she is talented. You both are different personalities, and need to be chiselled in different ways."

From that day forward, Qasim approached his practice with a new perspective. Years later, Qasim and Nadia both became master calligraphers.

Criticism is an inevitable part of life. Whether it comes from a boss, a colleague, a friend, or even a stranger, learning to handle criticism with grace is a vital skill that can help you grow both personally and professionally.

Criticism can generally be categorised into two types. The first type is often rooted in negativity, where the intent is to belittle, assert superiority, or stems from personal insecurities, jealousy, or ego. This kind of criticism usually serves the critic's need for validation or satisfaction in putting others down. It is best to ignore this type of criticism or harsh personal attacks, and not let them affect you. On the other hand, the second type of criticism is constructive feedback, aimed at bringing about an improvement. The key is to distinguish between the two – disregarding the former and accepting the latter with grace.

Regardless of its nature or delivery, criticism often triggers a defensive reaction. It is natural to feel hurt, angry, or embarrassed when faced with negative feedback. However, how we respond to criticism can significantly impact our personal growth and relationships.

Here are some practical steps to help you respond effectively to negative feedback.

Distinguish

The first step is to distinguish whether the criticism is aimed at putting you down or it is with the positive intent of bettering you. Once you have identified this, you are in a better position to decide whether you need to ignore or listen.

Listen actively

When someone criticises you, focus on listening carefully to their words without interrupting. Try to understand the core message and discern the intention behind it. Active listening demonstrates respect and helps you fully grasp the feedback being given.

Stay calm

It is easy to become defensive or emotional when receiving criticism. Take a few deep breaths to stay calm and composed. Keeping your emotions in check allows you to respond more thoughtfully and constructively.

Acknowledge the feedback

Show appreciation for constructive feedback, even if it is hard to hear. A simple "Thank you for your input" can go a long way in demonstrating that you value the critic's perspective.

Reflect before responding

Take some time to reflect on the criticism before responding. Consider whether there is truth to the feedback and how you can use it to improve yourself or your life. This reflection can help you respond more effectively and avoid knee-jerk reactions.

Ask for clarification

If the feedback is vague or unclear, do not hesitate to ask for clarification. Understanding specific details can help you address the issue more effectively.

Respond constructively

When you are ready to respond, do so constructively. Acknowledge any valid points and explain how you plan to address them. If you disagree with the feedback, express your perspective respectfully and seek a constructive dialogue.

Handling criticism with grace is about perspective. Instead of viewing criticism as a personal attack, see it as an opportunity for growth and learning. This shift in mindset can transform how you perceive and respond to feedback, leading to greater self-awareness and continuous improvement.

Criticism, though often uncomfortable, is a valuable tool for personal and professional progress. By learning to handle criticism with grace, you can transform negative feedback into positive change. Remember to listen actively, stay calm, and reflect before responding. Use feedback constructively, and maintain a growth-oriented outlook. In doing so, you will enhance your skills and relationships and build confidence in the face of life's challenges.

Golden Rule:

Transform criticism into growth by listening actively, staying calm, and using feedback constructively.

#39 | LET GO OF YOUR PAST

A teacher, aiming to teach his students about happiness, asked them to observe why people around them were unhappy. The students noticed that common reasons included regrets, guilt, resentment, anger, and hatred.

The teacher then instructed each student to bring a cloth bag and add a potato to it every time they themselves experienced these negative emotions. The condition was that they had to carry the bag with them everywhere. Initially, the task seemed easy, but over time, the bags grew heavier and the potatoes began to rot, causing discomfort and embarrassment.

A few days later, the teacher asked the students to gather and share their experiences. The students spoke about how their bags had become intolerable with the physical weight and the smell. The constant reminder of their negative emotions was overwhelming. They confessed how they had started to isolate themselves to avoid adding more potatoes to their bags, and more shame and embarrassment to themselves.

The teacher listened carefully to their stories and then spoke. "This is exactly how negative emotions from your past affect your life. They weigh you down, hinder your ability to move freely, and make it hard to enjoy life. Just as the potatoes have rotted and became a burden, so do these emotions, decaying within you and causing you constant pain."

He continued, "Now, imagine if instead of carrying these negative emotions, you chose to let them go, forgive others, forgive yourself, and focus on positive experiences and emotions. Your life would be much lighter and more pleasant."

The valuable wisdom the teacher wanted to impart to the students was that the past is a baggage we keep carrying, burdening our journey into the future. It slows us down and hinders our progress. However, it is within our power to let go of this weight and free ourselves from its grip. By releasing the burden of the past, we can pave the way for a more satisfying and successful future.

When we cling to past anger, guilt, regrets, resentments, and bad memories, we allow them to consume our present energy and time. These negative emotions hold us back, trapping us in a cycle of stagnation. We become stuck, unable to move forward and fully embrace life's possibilities.

To break free from this cycle, we must first acknowledge that the past cannot be changed. What is done is done, and no amount of dwelling on it can alter the course of events. Instead, we must redirect our focus towards the present moment and the opportunities it holds.

Letting go does not mean forgetting or denying our past. It means accepting it as part of our journey and using the lessons learnt to propel us forward. It means forgiving ourselves and others, understanding that we are all fallible beings who make mistakes.

Releasing the grip of the past requires a conscious effort. It may involve seeking closure, whether through conversations, or self-reflection. It also involves cultivating self-compassion and embracing a mindset of growth and resilience.

The secret of letting go is understanding that life will give you something much better than it is asking you to give up. To help you let go and create space in your life for the reality you desire, say these affirmations:

- I trust the journey and welcome change
- I release the past to embrace a brighter future
- I let go to create space for new blessings

As we let go of the baggage of the past, we create space for new experiences and possibilities. We become lighter, more adaptable, and open to the opportunities that come our way. Our journey through life becomes easier, as we no longer carry the weight of what cannot be changed.

The sooner we release and let go of the past that no longer serves us, the easier it is to move on to a brighter and joyful future.

Golden Rule:

Letting go of the past's burdens liberates us to embrace the present and create a happier future.

#40 | LIFE IS NOT A RACE

Let us revisit the famous story of the race between a hare and a tortoise. Here is the hare's version of the story.

Once upon a time, there was a speedy hare who was not lazy at all. He was so excited about the upcoming race that he could not sleep the whole night. Meanwhile, the tortoise boasted to everyone that he could walk for miles without stopping, saying life is like a long journey.

During the race, the hare found a cozy spot under a shady tree and a comfy rock covered with grass. But the peaceful atmosphere made him feel sleepy. He looked back and realised that the tortoise was far away and would take a while to catch up, and hence decided to take a nap. He drifted off and dreamt of sitting on a floating log in a beautiful stream, where he met an old hippopotamus wading calmly in the water. The old hippo asked the hare why he was racing.

"I want to prove I'm the fastest," the hare replied.

"But why?" the old hippo asked again.

"So that I can win a medal, be respected, and have lots of money and food," the hare explained.

"But there's plenty of food around you already," said the old hippo, looking at the fruit-laden trees. "And do you remember the names of the fastest deer, largest elephant, or strongest lion before you?"

The hare shook his head.

"Today, it's the tortoise challenging you. Tomorrow, it could be a snake, then a zebra. Will you keep running forever?" the old hippo questioned.

The hare pondered this. "Hmm... I never thought about it. I don't want to race my whole life."

"What do you want then?" the old hippo asked.

"I want to relax under a big tree, hop around meadows, and swim in ponds," the hare replied.

"You can do all that right now. Forget the race. You are here today, gone tomorrow," the old hippo advised, and waded away.

When the hare woke up, he saw ducks happily swimming in the pond and joined them. When asked about the race, he replied, "It's not important. I just want to be happy here."

Life is not a race. It is a journey meant to be enjoyed and experienced at one's own pace. In our fast-paced world, it is easy to feel pressured to constantly achieve, compete, and compare ourselves to others. We often find ourselves in a relentless pursuit of success, measuring our worth by how quickly we reach milestones or accumulate awards. However, this mindset can lead to burnout, stress, and a perpetual sense of lack. We keep on running after material wealth and success defined by others and, in the process, miss out completely on living life. Material wealth is essential for life, but it is not life.

Every person's path is different, and comparing our journey to others can rob us of the happiness that comes from personal growth and self-discovery. Life's true value lies in the experiences we have, the relationships we build, and the lessons we learn.

Embracing the idea that life is a unique journey allows us to appreciate the present moment, recognise our individual progress, and find joy in the small victories along the way.

By shifting our focus from the destination to the journey itself, we open ourselves up to a richer, more fulfilling existence. We begin to understand that it is not about how fast we achieve our goals, but about the meaningful moments and connections we make along the way. Embracing this perspective helps us to slow down, breathe, and truly live, rather than merely exist. We will be able to appreciate other types of wealth as well, such as sound sleep, good health, joyful laughter, close friends, trustworthy relations, and the time we spend with ourselves and our loved ones.

Remember, life is a journey to be relished at your own pace, not a race to be won by others' standards.

Golden Rule:

Life is not a race, it is a beautiful journey, so take a pause and enjoy every moment.

#41 | DECLUTTER FROM TIME TO TIME

Life in Banaras, also called Varanasi, is rich with traditions and spirituality. The narrow, winding streets are lined with old buildings full of history. The city is dotted with temples, where prayers and the scent of incense fill the air, reflecting a culture deeply connected to the divine.

Amidst this sacred backdrop, Banaras also has a rich culture of art and music. Musicians often sit by the riverbanks, creating soulful melodies that blend with the chants and temple bells, filling the air with an aura of devotion and calmness. The Banaras Gharana of Hindustani classical music is a distinguished tradition known for its distinctive style and rich musical heritage.

In one of the old buildings, there lived an elderly musician, renowned for his exquisite performances. People used to address him respectfully as Panditji. Panditji's small house was a sanctuary of sound, where every note exuded grace and clarity. Along with his work grew his collection of musical instruments, and with his fame grew the photographs of performances, gurus, and fellow musicians, alongside awards and certificates on the wall. Every inch of his house slowly began to fill up – hundreds of books on music on the shelves, and unfinished compositions in every corner, broken instruments mirroring chaos that seeped into his mind as well. This clutter had started reflecting in his compositions and performances, which had bothered him for some time now. The once sacred space lost its sanctity because of the clutter.

One day, a young student Swara joined Panditji, eager to learn the secrets of his craft. As she observed the disorder in his house, she hesitated but eventually voiced her concern, "Panditji, your music is so beautiful and serene, yet your surroundings are so messy. How do you find peace to create music?"

Panditji realised that this could be the reason that he was not enjoying his tranquil music anymore. He decided to take Swara's advice and help, and began a thorough cleaning. Together, they sorted through piles of material and discarded what was no longer needed. They organised the house, creating open spaces and bringing a sense of order.

As the physical clutter cleared, Panditji noticed a remarkable change within himself. His mind felt lighter, his thoughts more focused. With each day, he experienced a growing clarity that he had not felt in years. One evening, after weeks of cleaning, he sat down to create a new composition. In a short time, he created a new masterpiece, reflecting a profound sense of peace and harmony.

In the modern world, we accumulate a lot of clutter – both tangible and intangible. This clutter can weigh us down, cause stress, and hinder our ability to live fulfilling lives. Regularly decluttering, whether it is your physical space, mind or emotions, is essential for maintaining balance and achieving wellbeing.

Physical decluttering: Physical decluttering is not just about aesthetics; it profoundly impacts your daily life. A cluttered physical environment can make your space feel chaotic and difficult to navigate. Decluttering your physical space makes it more organised and functional, enhancing your daily routine. For example, imagine the ease of finding your keys on an organised key rack instead of searching through a pile of random items. A clutter-free environment positively impacts your mental health. Walking into a tidy, organised room can induce a sense of calm and order, reducing stress and promoting a peaceful state of mind. Physical decluttering also increases your efficiency.

Physical decluttering can start with small steps. Be honest about what you truly need and use, and let go of things that no longer serve you. Creating a system for organising your belongings can make a big difference. Regular maintenance is key. Make decluttering a regular habit by spending a few minutes each day tidying up.

Mental decluttering: In today's digital age, we are bombarded with information from all directions – news, social media and other content we engage in, reducing our efficacy and productivity. It induces stress and anxiety. It is important to declutter our mind on a daily basis and create space for clearer thinking and better focus.

Mental decluttering begins with practices such as mindfulness and meditation. These techniques help clear your mind and focus on the present moment. Imagine sitting quietly, focusing on your breath, and letting go of the myriad thoughts that usually crowd your mind. This practice can bring a sense of calm and clarity, making it easier to tackle tasks with a focused mindset.

Limit the information you take in. It is the processing of information that may drain your energy. Not everything you see or hear is important. Consume only what is important for your growth and success.

Writing things down is another effective strategy. Using a journal or planner to jot down tasks, thoughts, and ideas can help you organise your thoughts and reduce mental clutter. Think of it as emptying your mind on to paper, allowing you to see everything clearly and prioritise effectively. Setting priorities is crucial. By identifying your most important tasks and focusing on them first, you can avoid the overwhelm of trying to do everything at once. Avoid multitasking – it can increase mental clutter. Giving your full attention to one task at a time leads to better results.

Emotional decluttering: Emotional decluttering is equally important for maintaining emotional health. Holding on to negative emotions such as anger, resentment, or guilt can weigh you down, much like carrying around heavy luggage. Letting go of these feelings can lead to improved emotional wellbeing and a more positive outlook on life. For instance, consider how liberated it feels to forgive someone who has wronged you. By releasing these emotional burdens, you can experience a sense of relief and renewed positivity.

Emotional decluttering starts with acknowledging your feelings. Recognising and accepting your emotions, rather than suppressing them, is the first step towards letting go of negative feelings. Consider the catharsis of talking through your emotions with a trusted friend or therapist. Sharing your feelings can help you process and release them, leading to emotional relief.

Practising forgiveness, both for yourself and others, is another powerful way to declutter emotionally. Holding on to grudges and regrets only adds to emotional clutter. Forgiveness allows you to release these burdens and move forward with a lighter heart. Engage in self-care activities that nurture your emotional wellbeing, such as hobbies, exercise, or spending time in nature. These activities provide an outlet for emotional release and foster a sense of peace and happiness.

Digital decluttering: In today's times we also generate a lot of e-clutter. Excess files, spam emails and unnecessary apps eat away the space on your gadgets such as computers and mobile phones making them slow and less efficient. Deleting unnecessary data from time to time should become a habit for better performance.

Make decluttering a consistent practice, and you will experience the profound benefits it brings to your overall wellbeing. With a clear mind, a light heart, and an organised space, you can steer life more smoothly and enjoy the journey to the fullest.

Golden Rule:

Decluttering regularly brings in focus and reduces stress, while improving relationships and enhancing peace and calm.

#42 | RESPOND, NOT REACT

In a busy city, a well-known chef Sofia ran a restaurant that was frequented by many food lovers. She was famous not only for her culinary skills but also her cool demeanour. However, one day, her patience was tested.

That morning, Sofia arrived at her restaurant to find a mysterious note taped to the front door. The note read: "Your food is overrated and overpriced. I've had better meals at fast-food joints. You should quit cooking."

Sofia's first instinct was to publicly denounce the critic or vent out her frustration. But then, she remembered the advice her grandmother had given her: "Respond, don't react. Wisdom lies in understanding before acting."

She took a deep breath, folded the note, and put it in her pocket. That evening Sofia shared the note with her staff and asked for their thoughts. One of her waiters mentioned a particular customer who had complained about the waiting time the previous night.

Sofia found the name of the customer in the reservations register. Instead of reacting with anger, she chose to respond with empathy. She wrote a personal letter to the critic, expressing regret for their disappointing experience and offering a complimentary meal to show the true quality of her restaurant.

A few days later, the same customer returned. This time, Sofia personally made sure that the service was swift and the food was perfect. The critic, initially wary, was soon won over by Sofia's genuine hospitality. After the dinner, the customer came up to Sofia and apologised for the harsh note. He admitted that he had been having a rough day and had unfairly taken it out on her restaurant. He praised her for handling the situation with grace and acknowledged that her food was, indeed, extraordinary.

By choosing to respond thoughtfully rather than react impulsively, Sofia not only saved her restaurant's reputation but also turned a critic into a loyal customer.

In a world that often demands instant replies and snap judgements, the distinction between reacting and responding becomes crucial. A reaction is immediate, often driven by emotion and impulse, while responding involves a thoughtful consideration of the situation. It is not the external events in our life that disturb us, but our own reactions to them.

Reacting is automatic, triggered by an event or a provocation. It is instinctive, often without a rational thought. While this can be advantageous in situations requiring quick reflexes, it can be damaging in relationships where thoughtful communication is key. Reactions are normally fuelled by strong emotions like anger, fear, or frustration.

Responding, in contrast, involves a process of thinking through a situation before acting. It requires self-control, reflection, and often empathy, leading to more measured actions. Responses consider the potential outcomes of actions. They aim to address the root of the issue and find a positive solution. Responding brings in healthier communication, reducing misunderstandings and conflicts. It builds trust and respect, as others feel heard and valued.

Imagine a colleague criticises your work in a meeting. A reaction might be to defend yourself angrily or criticise them in return. A response, however, would involve acknowledging their feedback, reflecting on its validity, and addressing any issues calmly and constructively.

In a heated argument with a loved one, reacting might mean shouting or saying hurtful things. Responding involves taking a deep breath, listening to their point of view, and expressing your feelings without escalating the conflict.

By taking time to think through actions, responses are more likely to be logical and effective, leading to better outcomes in both personal and professional scenarios. Responding reduces stress and anxiety, as it involves managing emotions rather than being overwhelmed by them. It promotes a sense of control and calm.

Here are few ways to cultivate responding:

Self-awareness: The first step is developing self-awareness. Recognise your emotional triggers and the situations that prompt immediate reactions.

Pause and breathe: Before reacting, take a moment to pause and breathe. This short break allows you to gather your thoughts and calm your mind. Never react when you are Hurt, Angry, Lonely, and Tired (HALT).

Reflect: Consider the situation from different angles. Ask yourself questions like:

- What am I feeling right now?
- Why am I feeling this way?
- What is the best way to handle this situation?
- What are the potential consequences of my action?

Empathy and understanding: Put yourself in the other person's shoes. Try to understand their perspective and emotions. This can diffuse tension and lead to more compassionate responses.

Listen and speak clearly: Be a good listener and be assertive while speaking. This helps in expressing your thoughts clearly and respectfully, leading to more constructive conversations.

Whether dealing with unexpected challenges at work, conflicts in relationships, or simply navigating through daily challenges, our response makes all the difference. By becoming more self-aware, taking time to reflect, and cultivating empathy, you can transform your interactions and make more thoughtful, positive contributions to any situation. This shift from reaction to response not only improves your relationships and decision-making but also enhances your emotional wellbeing, leading to a more balanced and satisfying life.

Golden Rule:

In every interaction, choose thoughtful response over impulsive reaction. How we choose to respond in a situation will shape our outcomes and relationships.

#43 | NEVER EVER LET GO OF YOURSELF

A little boy Karan came home from school and excitedly told his father, "My teacher gave us homework to hug 10 people and tell them, 'Keep faith, be patient, and I love you.'"

His dad replied, "Okay, we'll go to the mall tomorrow morning and do it."

Karan woke up full of energy the next morning, got ready, and eagerly said, "Let's go."

His father hesitated. "It's raining heavily, and I'm worried no one will be there."

But Karan insisted, so his father drove through the pouring rain to the mall. They spent an hour there, and Karan managed to hug nine people.

His father then said, "Now let's go; it's raining heavily, and we shouldn't get stuck in traffic."

Feeling a bit disheartened but obedient, Karan agreed. As they were driving home, Karan pointed to a random house and pleaded, "Please, dad, just one more person. I need to complete my homework."

His father smiled and pulled the car over. Karan ran to the door and knocked vigorously. After a long wait, the door slowly opened.

A lady appeared, looking very sad, and gently asked, "What can I do for you, son?"

With shining eyes and a bright smile, Karan said, "Ma'am, my teacher told us to hug 10 people and tell them, 'Keep faith, be patient, and I love you.' I have hugged nine. May I hug you and pass on the message?"

The lady embraced him and started crying profusely.

Seeing this, Karan 's father got out of the car and approached her. "Is everything okay, madam?" he asked.

She composed herself, invited them inside, and offered them tea. She then shared her story. "My husband died some time ago, leaving me completely alone. This morning, the loneliness overwhelmed me. I decided that today would be the end. I took a chair and a rope to my bedroom, planning to end my life. Just as I was preparing to say goodbye to the world, I heard a knock. I almost ignored it because no one ever visits me. But then I decided to answer. When I opened the door, I saw this little boy. And when he said, 'Keep faith, be patient, and I love you,' I knew it was a message from the universe. Suddenly, I realised I did not want to die anymore. I must find a new purpose in life."

Even in your darkest times, the universe is always guiding and protecting you. When the universe does not let go of you, why should you let go of yourself?

Trust that the trials and tribulations you encounter are mere stepping stones towards growth and self-discovery. The universe conspires in mysterious ways to guide you towards your destiny, and it is up to you to grasp those opportunities and forge your own path.

Amidst all the chaos and uncertainties of life, there is one person who remains constant and ever-present – you. You are the most important person in your life. It is crucial to stand up for who you are, for your dreams, aspirations, values, and even your failures. Ups and downs are an inevitable part of the journey, but never let yourself go, and never let yourself down.

Embracing the essence of your being, with all its flaws and imperfections, is the key to unlocking your true potential. Have faith in yourself, for it is this unwavering belief that will always pull you up when you stumble and fall. When the world tries to push you down, remember that if not you, then who else will stand up for you?

From the moment you take your first breath to the moment you depart from this world, it is your individual journey. So, you must always believe that you are worthy, enough, and complete in all respects. It is only when you look up to yourself and respect the person you have become that the world will look up to you in return.

What you think of yourself is more important than what other people think about you. Do not let yourself down by internalising other people's opinions about you. Always watch your inner dialogue.

Create positive belief systems by way of repeating affirmations. For instance, you may say, "I am always divinely guided and protected," "I am successful in whatever I do", "I am the best", or "I love and approve of myself unconditionally."

If you are going through humongous challenges and the future seems dark, believe in the mantra, "This too shall pass." Understand the deeper meaning in every experience, challenge or change that you go through.

Never lose hope because hope gives you the ability to bounce back from adversities. Never let the outer storm take away your inner peace. Change your perspective about yourself. This will help you raise your self-worth.

You are the protagonist of your own story. The world awaits the magnificence that lies within you, and it is time to let it shine.

Golden Rule:

Even in your darkest times, trust that the universe is guiding you, and never let go of yourself.

#44 | LEARN TO SAY NO

Long ago, there was a legendary archer named Kritidutta. His skill with the bow and arrow was unmatched, and everyone sought his help to solve their problems, whether it was hunting dangerous beasts or protecting the village from robbers. Kritidutta was a kind-hearted man who found it difficult to refuse anyone's request. He believed that saying 'no' was impolite and unkind, so he always agreed to every help everyone, no matter how difficult it was for him at times.

People began to expect that Kritidutta would always be available to help, which increased the demands on his time. He soon found himself overburdened and exhausted, his focus suffering in the process. He lost the joy he once got from his passion, due to stress and obligation. Kritidutta's effectiveness as an archer diminished. He could not give his best to any single task, which reduced the impact of his efforts and the quality of the help he provided.

One day, an old sage visited Kritidutta and observed his weariness. The sage asked him, "Why do you agree to every request? Do you believe you are the only one who can help these people?" Kritidutta was taken aback, but realised the truth in the sage's words. Kritidutta explained his difficulty, expressing his reluctance to refuse anyone. The sage continued, "By saying 'yes' to everything, you are depleting your strength and compromising your true potential. Learn to say 'no' when necessary, so you can say 'yes' to what truly matters."

Kritidutta took the sage's advice to heart. He began to prioritise his commitments, focusing on tasks where his skills were most needed, and saying 'no' to those that others could handle. This change allowed him to maintain his exceptional abilities and provide the best help possible when it was truly needed.

In time, Kritidutta reached new heights of excellence, and he became even more renowned for his archery. He learnt that saying 'no' when necessary was not a sign of weakness or unkindness, but a way to protect his passion and deliver his best work.

From an early age, we are conditioned to view saying 'no' as rude and potentially hurtful to others. We are taught to prioritise the needs and expectations of those around us, often at the expense of our own wellbeing. However, this habit of always saying 'yes' can create a foundation for people-pleasing, which can become difficult to break as we get older.

What if I told you that saying 'no' is actually one of the most valuable things you can do for yourself? When you master the ability to assertively say 'no', you reclaim your autonomy and establish healthy boundaries. You no longer rely on others to validate your self-worth, nor do you feel obligated to please others at your own expense.

By saying 'no', you prioritise your own needs, desires, and goals. You gain the courage to decline opportunities or commitments that do not align with your values or aspirations. This newfound assertiveness empowers you to make choices that are in line with your authentic self, fostering a sense of integrity and personal fulfilment.

Identify the situations that leave you drained, or people who overstep or your limits in other areas. The next step is to set boundaries. Setting boundaries through saying 'no' is an act of self-care and self-respect. It communicates that you value your time, energy, and resources, and that you are not willing to compromise them for the sake of others' expectations. As a result, you experience a sense of empowerment and freedom that comes from knowing that you are in control of your own decisions and actions.

Learning to say 'no' also helps cultivate meaningful and mutually respectful relationships. When you establish clear boundaries, you attract people who appreciate and respect your honesty. True connections are built on authenticity and understanding, rather than on the constant need to please others. Saying 'no' allows you to create space for healthier and more fulfilling interactions.

Of course, saying 'no' can be challenging at first. It requires practice and self-reflection. Start by recognising and questioning the underlying beliefs and fears that hold you back from saying 'no'. Understand that saying 'no' is not selfish or mean. Say it politely but firmly. It is an act of self-preservation, self-care, loving yourself and putting yourself first.

As you begin to say 'no' more often, you will likely face resistance and pushback from others. Stay firm in your conviction and remind yourself of the importance of your wellbeing. Surround yourself with supportive individuals who understand and respect your boundaries.

Remember, by learning to say 'no', you create the space to say 'yes' to the things that truly matter to you. You reclaim your power and embrace a life that is guided by your own choices.

So, practice the art of saying 'no' assertively and confidently, and watch your sense of self-worth soar.

Golden Rule:

Saying 'no' assertively and confidently is an act of self-care and empowerment that enables you to prioritise your own self and aligns your life with your true values and aspirations.

#45 | LEARN TO LIVE WITH UNCERTAINTY

In a remote village situated in the foothills of the Himalayas, there was a river that flowed through the heart of the settlement. The villagers depended on the river for their livelihood, drawing water for their crops and fishing in its abundant waters. However, this river was notorious for its unpredictability. In some seasons, it would flood, sweeping away everything in its path, while at other times it would dry up, leaving the land parched.

One year, the river's unpredictability was particularly severe. The village elders called a meeting to discuss how to cope with the uncertain nature of their lifeline. They invited an old wanderer sage, who had lived through many such uncertainties and was famed for his wisdom.

During the meeting, one of the young villagers stood up and voiced his frustration. "How can we build our lives around this river when it constantly changes? How can we plan for the future with such uncertainty?"

The sage smiled and suggested that instead of fighting the river's changes, they should learn to adapt to them. He advised the villagers to build movable structures like floating platforms for their homes, so that they could quickly relocate during floods. He told them how they could store water during dry spells by developing new irrigation techniques to make the most of the river's changing flow; and also to diversify their crops to ensure they had food even in the harshest conditions. But most importantly, he taught them to find joy in the present moment, rather than constantly worrying about the future.

Over time, the villagers thrived not because the river became predictable, but because they embraced its unpredictability. They learnt to live with uncertainty by becoming flexible and strong. They realised that the river's changes were not obstacles, but opportunities to grow stronger and more resourceful.

In time, the village not only survived but thrived. The villagers learnt that uncertainty, when embraced with an open heart and a flexible mind, could lead to unexpected and remarkable growth.

Uncertainty is an inevitable part of the human experience. It is something we all encounter at various stages of our lives; in our careers, relationships and in many other aspects of life.

Learning to live with uncertainty is a valuable skill that can help us navigate the unpredictable nature of life with grace and courage. Here's how you can do it.

1. The first step is accepting uncertainty as a natural aspect of life. It is perfectly okay to not have all the answers or know what the future holds. By acknowledging this, we release the burden of trying to control every aspect of our lives and open ourselves up to new possibilities.
2. Instead of dwelling on the uncertainties, direct your attention and energy towards the present moment. By staying grounded in the here and now, you can alleviate unnecessary worry about the future and rumination about the past.
3. Indulge in practices such as meditation, exercise, or engaging in activities that bring you joy and relaxation. These techniques will help you cultivate a sense of inner calm and peace, even in the face of uncertainty.
4. Surround yourself with a supportive network of family, friends, or mentors who can provide guidance and encouragement during uncertain times.
5. Adopt a solution-oriented mindset. Instead of brooding over the problems uncertainty throws at you, always try to find a solution to the problem in question.

Reframe uncertainty as an opportunity for growth and learning. **Challenges and unexpected situations are valuable teachers.** They provide us with the chance to develop resilience, adaptability, and problem-solving skills. Embracing a mindset of flexibility allows us to navigate uncertainty with greater ease.

Remember, no matter how meticulously we plan, life may throw unexpected situations at us. Learning to live with uncertainty means accepting that not everything will go as planned. Embrace the journey of adapting to the unforeseen. Do not take anything for granted, as everything can change in a moment. Be grateful for all that you have and all that you are. Life is a gift and we are truly blessed.

Golden Rule:

Embrace uncertainty as an opportunity for growth and new possibilities.

#46 TREAT OTHERS AS YOU WISH TO BE TREATED

In the picturesque town of Willowbrook, surrounded by hills and lush forests, there was a peculiar shop called Serenity Emporium. It wasn't just any store. It was a place of wisdom, where the shopkeeper, an enigmatic figure named Evander, shared profound insights with those who sought his guidance.

On a particularly chilly evening, as the sun dipped below the horizon, a troubled soul named Maya wandered into the Serenity Emporium. Her heart weighed heavy with regret, and her mind was clouded with guilt.

Evander, with his calm demeanour and piercing gaze, greeted Maya with a warm smile. "Welcome, dear traveller. What burdens weigh upon your soul today?"

Maya hesitated for a moment before pouring out her troubles to Evander. She recounted a recent incident where her actions had caused harm to another person. "I never meant to hurt anyone," she said, her voice trembling with remorse.

Evander listened attentively, his wise eyes reflecting empathy and understanding. After Maya had finished speaking, he gently placed a hand on her shoulder and spoke in a soothing tone. "My dear Maya, you have stumbled upon a fundamental truth of existence – one that is as old as time itself. It is the principle of never causing harm to another soul."

He gestured toward a dusty book resting on a nearby shelf and continued, "In the ancient texts of wisdom it is written, 'Do unto others as you would have them do unto you.' This simple yet profound proverb forms the cornerstone of moral conduct across cultures and civilisations."

Maya nodded, her eyes glistening with tears. "But what can I do now? How can I make amends for the pain I have caused?" Evander smiled reassuringly. "The path to redemption begins with genuine remorse and a sincere desire to correct the wrongs we have committed. It is not enough to simply regret our actions. We must take concrete steps to repair the damage and prevent such harm from occurring again."

He guided Maya through a series of reflective exercises, encouraging her to empathise with the person she had hurt and to envisage ways in which she could offer amends. Together, they crafted a plan of action rooted in kindness, compassion, and forgiveness. As Maya left the Serenity Emporium that evening, a sense of hope blossomed within her heart. Though the road to redemption would not be easy, she carried with her the invaluable lesson shared by Evander.

In the days that followed, Maya embarked on a journey of self-discovery and healing. Maya learnt the timeless truth – that the greatest strength lies not in causing harm, but in showing compassion; not in tearing others down, but in lifting them up. Inflicting harm on others disregards their feelings, experiences, and wellbeing. Instead, by cultivating empathy and compassion, we can recognise the inherent worth and dignity of every individual, leading to more harmonious relationships.

The golden rule, present in various cultures and religions, emphasises treating others as we wish to be treated, creating mutual respect, understanding, and cooperation. **If you hurt someone, you are hurt too, ending up in long-term distress.** The concept of karma teaches that our actions have consequences. By choosing kindness over cruelty, we sow seeds of positivity and goodwill, enriching our lives and the lives of others.

If we accidentally hurt someone, it is important to say sorry and try to make things right again. Here are some ways to do this.

Acknowledge the hurt

Understand what you did to cause hurt. Reflect on your actions, words, and the impact they had. Accept that your actions caused pain without making excuses or blaming others.

Apologise sincerely

Choose an appropriate time and private setting to have a meaningful conversation. Start with a sincere apology, clearly stating that you are sorry for what you did.

Listen and validate

Give the other person a chance to express their feelings without interrupting. Show empathy by acknowledging their pain and frustration.

Make amends

Ask the person what you can do to make amends or repair the harm. Be open to their suggestions.

Change behaviour

Understand why the hurtful behaviour happened and work on changing it to prevent future occurrences.

Give it time

Healing takes time. Allow the other person to process and heal at their own pace.

By considering how our actions and words might affect others, we create an environment of understanding and kindness. This principle encourages us to step into another person's shoes, promoting a sense of compassion and shared humanity. When we treat others with the same consideration and respect we desire for ourselves, we contribute to building stronger, more harmonious relationships.

Living by this principle can profoundly impact both our personal and professional lives. In personal relationships, it helps cultivate trust and emotional safety. When we show kindness, patience, and respect to our family and friends, we create a supportive and loving atmosphere.

In the professional realm, treating colleagues, clients, and employees with respect and fairness fosters a positive work environment. It enhances collaboration, boosts morale, and increases productivity. When people feel valued and respected, they are more likely to be motivated and engaged in their work.

Ultimately, treating others as we wish to be treated is not just about kindness but about recognising our shared human experience. It reminds us that our actions have the power to uplift and inspire those around us, creating a ripple effect of positivity and respect that extends beyond individual interactions. By embracing this principle, we contribute to a more compassionate and connected world.

Golden Rule:

Live with empathy and kindness, treating others as you wish to be treated, to create a ripple of positivity and respect in the world.

#47 | BE GOOD AT ASKING FOR HELP

Little Kian was playing in a sandpit in the backyard of his house. He was creating roads and tunnels in the sand with the help of his plastic pail and a shiny, yellow plastic shovel. He was going to put his collection of tiny cars and trucks on these roads. Kian's father was watching his son play from his living room.

In the process of creating roads and tunnels in the soft sand, Kian found that there was a large rock in the middle of the sandpit. The little boy dug around the rock, managing to take it out of the sand. With a little struggle, he pushed the large rock across the sandpit by using his feet.

When Kian got the rock to the edge of the sandpit, he found that he could not roll it out of the pit as there was a steep slope.

Determined, the little boy pushed, but every time he thought he had made some progress, the rock tipped and fell back into the sandpit. Kian struggled, pushed, and shoved, but his only reward was to have the rock roll back in the pit. In the end, he burst into tears of frustration.

Kian's father, who was watching this drama unfold, came to him and said, "Son, why didn't you use all the strength that you had available?"

Kian, now sobbing, replied, "But I did, daddy. I used all the strength that I had."

"No, son," corrected the father gently. "You did not use all the strength you had. You did not ask me." Saying this, the father reached down, picked up the rock and removed it from the sandpit.

We all have 'rocks' in our life that need to be removed; it is just that the 'rocks' take different forms for each one of us. When we discover that we are not able to lift a rock single-handedly, there is always someone such as a loved one or a friend who is willing to give us the strength we need.

One of the biggest mistakes we make in life is trying to do everything alone. We often believe that asking for help is a sign of weakness. However, there is nothing wrong in asking for help. In reality, it takes a lot of strength and courage to admit that we cannot do something alone. **Asking for help when we need it can make our lives easier, faster, and more efficient.**

Seeking help saves time and effort. It enables us to tap into someone else's knowledge and experience, benefitting from their expertise and avoiding unnecessary mistakes. By reaching out to others, we can leverage their skills and perspectives to overcome challenges and achieve our goals more effectively.

Moreover, asking for help builds relationships. When we ask someone for help, we show that we trust and respect them. It fosters a sense of solidarity and creates opportunities for partnership. By involving others in our journey, we strengthen our connections and create a support network that can uplift us in times of need. It humbles us and allows us to learn from others. It requires us to be vulnerable and open-minded, setting aside our pride and embracing the support that others can offer.

You will be amazed to see how many people would be ready and happy to help you, if you ask them.

Golden Rule:

True strength lies in recognising when we need help and having the courage to ask for it.

#48 | TAKE CARE OF YOURSELF

I had not seen my father's friend, Mr Patel, for many years and had lost touch with him after my father passed away. One day, out of the blue, I received a phone call from Mr Patel. He expressed a desire to see me.

When I visited him, I could not believe what I saw. I was in total shock. Here was a man who had climbed the ladder of success, accumulated great wealth, and reached the pinnacle of his career. His home was filled with luxuries that many could only dream of, and he had accomplished feats that inspired all who knew him. Yet, despite his remarkable achievements, there was one crucial aspect he had neglected – his health.

Mr Patel had dedicated his life to his work, often sacrificing sleep, proper meals, and exercise in his relentless pursuit of success. Over time, his body bore the brunt of this neglect. One day, he suffered a severe stroke, leaving him paralysed and confined to a wheelchair. It was heart-wrenching to see a man who had once been so dynamic and vibrant now unable to enjoy the luxuries he had worked so hard for.

This experience taught me a profound lesson – if health is lost, everything is lost. **No amount of wealth or success can compensate for a body that is unable to function.** Our body is the vehicle that carries us through life, and it deserves our utmost care and attention.

Given below are the essential elements that can help you live a healthy life.

Food

Imagine your body as a finely tuned machine, requiring quality fuel to operate at its best. Just like a car needs the right type of gasoline, your body thrives on simple, wholesome food. Opt for fresh fruits, vegetables, lean proteins, and whole grains. These foods provide essential nutrients that support your body's functions, boost your energy levels, and promote overall wellbeing.

In the modern world, our busy schedules often lead us to compromise on our diet. Many of us frequently turn to fast food, skip meals, or grab whatever is convenient. While we might not notice the impact of these habits when we are young, the toll on our bodies becomes apparent as we age, manifesting in various health issues.

Hydration

Similarly, staying hydrated is vital for maintaining optimal health. Water is your body's primary building block, essential for digestion, circulation, temperature regulation, and waste removal. Drink plenty of water throughout the day to keep your body functioning smoothly and efficiently. I generally tend to forget to drink water if I am occupied, so I downloaded an app which reminds me that I must drink water at set intervals.

Restful sleep

Sleep is your body's time for rejuvenation and repair. During sleep, your body heals tissues, consolidates memories, and regulates hormones. Aim for seven to nine hours of restful sleep each night by establishing a consistent bedtime routine and creating a comfortable sleep environment.

We often burn the midnight oil, neglecting sleep in favour of more work or in today's world we indulge in binge-watching. The cumulative effect of chronic sleep deprivation finally takes a toll on our health and disturbs our circadian rhythms.

Circadian rhythms are 24-hour cycles that are part of the body's internal clock, running in the background to carry out essential functions and processes. Keeping a consistent routine and sleep schedule can maintain a healthy circadian rhythm. Sleeping at the right time is just as important as the number of hours of sleep.

Movement

In addition to rest, your body also craves movement. Regular exercise is key to maintaining a healthy body and mind. Whether it is a leisurely walk in nature, a yoga class, or a high-intensity workout, find activities that you enjoy and make them a regular part of your routine. Movement not only strengthens your muscles and improves your cardiovascular health, but also boosts your mood and reduces stress. Mr Patel's sedentary lifestyle contributed to his physical decline. Regular physical activity might have prevented some of the health issues he faced.

Laughter

Laughter truly is the best medicine for your body and soul. Laughter releases endorphins, your body's natural feel-good chemicals, which can reduce stress, boost your mood, and improve your immune function. Surround yourself with people and activities that bring joy and laughter into your life.

Social connections

Social connections are equally important for your overall well-being. Cultivate meaningful relationships with friends and loved ones who support and uplift you. Spend time together, share experiences, and lean on each other during difficult times. Remember that laughter and friendship go hand in hand, creating a strong foundation for your mental and emotional health.

Avoid stress

Stress is the root cause of many physical and mental illnesses. Stress is a modern pandemic that has gripped one and all irrespective of the age group. Chronic stress can lead to a host of physical and mental health issues, including heart disease, high blood pressure, anxiety, and depression. To minimise stress, it is important to identify triggers and to develop a positive perspective or mindset. Coping strategies may include practising relaxation techniques, meditation, or yoga, which can help reduce the body's physiological response to stressors.

Mind your mind

Taking care of your mind is as crucial as taking care of your body. A healthy mind enables us to navigate life's challenges with strength, maintain emotional balance, and experience a deeper sense of joy. One effective way to care for your mind is through meditation. Regular meditation to connect to your deeper self encourages you to focus on the present moment, reducing stress and anxiety. It has shown to improve concentration, manage emotions, and promote a sense of calm. By setting aside a few minutes each day to meditate, you can cultivate a habit that supports mental clarity and emotional stability. You can choose an effective breathing technique such as SKY Healing that helps you heal both body and emotions, and does not require much time to practise. Or you can meditate through any other induction techniques such as progressive relaxation or visualisation.

Digital detox

Constant exposure to digital information and greater screen time can lead to overstimulation of the brain, resulting in mental fatigue, stress, and overwhelm. Our brains are constantly bombarded with notifications, emails, social-media updates, and news, leaving little room for quiet contemplation and creative thinking. This makes it most important to do a digital detox regularly. By disconnecting from technology, you give yourself a chance to recharge and regain focus. This break from technology allows your mind to wander, daydream, and make unexpected connections.

One effective way to do a digital detox is to select a day in a week when you consciously switch off your data and WiFi (keeping your phone on for emergency purposes). Instead, dedicate that time to reconnect with nature or engage in activities you love doing. Take a walk in the park, hike a trail, or simply sit by a serene lake. **Engage in activities that allow you to be present in the moment and appreciate the wonders of the physical world.** Or you can spend quality time with your loved ones or with yourself.

By taking a break from technology, you give yourself the opportunity to recharge, reset, and gain a new perspective. You will find that this intentional disconnection not only boosts your creativity but also enhances your overall wellbeing.

Your body and mind are your most precious assets, and they deserve care, respect, and appreciation. By nourishing your body with wholesome food, staying hydrated, prioritising restful sleep, engaging in regular movement, sharing laughter with others, and nurturing meaningful relationships, you can optimise your health and vitality for the journey ahead. Taking care of your mind is a continuous process that requires attention and effort, but the rewards are well worth it.

Golden Rule:

Take good care of your body and mind and keep them healthy to live a happy and joyful life.

#49 | NEVER STOP LEARNING AND GROWING

Why are we here? This question has puzzled philosophers, theologians, and thinkers throughout the ages. One compelling answer is that we are here to learn and evolve. Every experience, good or bad, joyous or painful, is an opportunity for growth. Through learning, we gain insights into ourselves, others, and the world around us. We discover our strengths and confront our weaknesses. We learn to navigate the complexities of life with greater wisdom and compassion.

Not all lessons come from grand or tragic events. Many of life's most profound teachings come from everyday moments. A conversation with a stranger can teach us about kindness. A walk in nature can remind us of the beauty and interconnectedness of all life. The mundane tasks of daily life, when approached with mindfulness, can become rich with learning. These small lessons accumulate, shaping us in subtle but significant ways.

To fully embrace life's lessons, we must cultivate a growth mindset.

This means viewing challenges as opportunities, not obstacles. It means being open to feedback and willing to make mistakes. A growth mindset allows us to see every experience, no matter how difficult, as a chance to learn and grow. It transforms our approach to life, making us more adaptable, strong, and curious.

Learning from life requires reflection. It is not enough to simply go through experiences; we must take the time to reflect on them. What did we learn? How did we grow? What can we do differently next time? Reflection helps us internalise the lessons we have learnt and apply them to future situations. It turns experience into wisdom.

The world we live in has so much to offer. There is no end to learning and growing. We just need to be curious. **When we approach life with curiosity, we are constantly seeking to understand more, to explore new ideas, and to expand our horizons.** Curiosity leads us down paths we might never have considered, opening up a world of possibilities.

During times of change or transformation, it is natural to feel scared or insecure. Every significant change involves letting go of the old to embrace the new. This is a universal experience, and it is a vital part of discovering who we truly are. Stay strong, keep your heart open, and trust that you are evolving into the incredible person you are meant to be.

Another interesting fact I have observed is that the universe has a way of presenting us with the same situations repeatedly until we learn the lessons they are meant to teach. This cyclical pattern is not a sign of failure but an opportunity for growth and self-awareness. When we find ourselves in familiar, often challenging circumstances, it is a call to examine our reactions, thoughts, and behaviours. The discomfort we feel is a signal that change is necessary. It is through these recurring experiences that we are given the chance to develop new perspectives and approaches, ultimately leading to personal transformation.

Also, old habits, no matter how ingrained, do not open new doors. They keep us stuck in a cycle of repetition, preventing us from reaching our full potential. To evolve and grow, we must recognise and eliminate these limiting patterns. Embracing new habits allows us to step into a future where we can thrive and realise our true potential.

The Power of Change

If you feel that you are stuck in a particular environment and feel that your growth has stagnated due to this, it is better to change your surroundings. Changing your environment can have a profound impact on personal growth and development. When we alter our surroundings, we open ourselves up to new experiences, perspectives, and opportunities that can inspire and challenge us in ways we never imagined. This shift can break the monotony of our daily routines and stimulate creativity and innovation, pushing us to step out of our comfort zones and embrace growth.

One of the key benefits of changing your environment is the

exposure to different cultures, ideas, and ways of thinking. Whether it is moving to a new city, travelling to a foreign country, or simply joining a new community or group, these experiences can broaden our horizons and help us see the world from different viewpoints. This exposure not only enhances our understanding and empathy towards others but also encourages us to question our own beliefs and assumptions, leading to personal growth and development.

A change in environment can help us break free from negative patterns and habits that may be holding us back. It can also reignite your passion and motivation. When we find ourselves stuck in a rut, a new environment can provide the fresh start we need to rediscover our purpose and enthusiasm for life.

The Power of Consistency

The power of small, positive changes, repeated consistently over time, is immense. Just as a single drop of water, when falling consistently over time, can cut through a rock, tiny habits, when practised regularly, can lead to significant transformations in our lives. This concept is often referred to as the "compound effect", where incremental improvements accumulate to create profound, lasting change. **By integrating small, positive habits into our daily routine, we set the stage for personal growth and a more fulfilling life.**

One of the key advantages of adopting small habits is their manageability. Large goals can often feel overwhelming and unattainable, leading to procrastination and discouragement.

In contrast, small changes are easier to implement and maintain, reducing the psychological barrier to starting. Dedicating just a few minutes each day to reading, meditation, or learning a new skill can accumulate into a wealth of knowledge and personal development.

Discipline and consistency play a crucial role in this process. It is not just about making changes; it's about sticking with them over the long haul. Consistent effort, no matter how small, builds momentum and creates a sense of accomplishment that fuels further progress. This discipline helps in forming habits, which then become second nature.

Life is not a destination but a journey. Along this journey, every step, every turn, and every pause holds meaning. By learning the lessons that life offers, we continue to grow, evolve, and fulfil our purpose. We become more than we were yesterday, inching closer to the best versions of ourselves. This journey of learning and evolving is what gives life its richness and depth.

Golden Rule:

Embrace every experience as an opportunity to learn and grow, for it is through life's lessons that we discover our true potential and purpose.

#50 | LIVE LIFE TO THE FULLEST

Geeta lost her husband after 10 years of marriage when she was just 35. Her world fell apart as she had no job and two daughters to care for. Though she had a postgraduate degree in computer science, she had chosen to be a homemaker. The sudden change in her circumstances forced her to enter the workforce. Over time, her daughters graduated and became independent. By then, Geeta was almost 50 and found herself struggling with the empty-nest syndrome, feeling a profound loss of purpose and sinking into depression.

Fortunately, she found a mentor who guided her to rediscover herself. Geeta had always had a passion for dancing. She began creating dance reels and posting them on social media, but faced harsh criticism. People made cruel comments, saying, "This is not the age to dance; you should spend your time in prayers," and, "Do you want to break your knees, lady?"

Despite the trolling and humiliation, Geeta decided to live her life on her terms. She pursued her childhood dreams and took up trekking, biking, and cycling, covering great distances.

Geeta is a shining example of how to live life to the fullest. She expressed herself through dance and explored the length and breadth of the country, showing that it is never too late to follow your passions and find a purpose to your life.

When we are vulnerable, there is a possibility that things will go differently than we had planned, but it is crucial to experiencing life in a full, open, honest way. It also brings spontaneity to life, making it interesting.

When we embrace who we are, including our imperfections, we allow ourselves to fully experience life. Accepting ourselves means letting go of our fears, doubts, and societal expectations that often hold us back. It means recognising that it is okay to be flawed, to get wet in the rain, to feel scared, and to let our inner child come out and play.

Once, when it was raining in Mumbai, we had some guests over and decided to trek to a 2,000-year-old Buddhist cave, located about six kilometres from our house. The idea thrilled the two kids amongst us, while the adults came up with various excuses. However, the kids' excitement was infectious, persuading the adults to join in. A few were still wary and insisted on bringing umbrellas, but the rest of us ventured out in the rain without any protection. We were all drenched before even reaching the caves. As the trek began, our inhibitions melted away. We danced in puddles, raced each other, revelled in the waterfalls, and shouted with both excitement and fear. Reaching the cave's summit, we were greeted with a breathtaking view. There was a profound sense of contentment, achievement and smiles on everyone's face.

It is important to get out of your comfort zone, venture out and embrace the unknown. You may not really know what you are capable of unless you try it.

Travel expands your horizons, offering new perspectives and experiences that enrich life in countless ways. It opens doors to different cultures, languages, and landscapes, aiding personal growth and deepening your understanding of the world. Whether exploring bustling cities, serene natural wonders, or engaging with diverse communities, each journey brings moments of discovery and adventure. Travelling widely not only rejuvenates the spirit but also broadens the mind, allowing you to live life to its fullest.

Recently, I visited a hospital in Mumbai where my mother-in-law underwent surgery. There, I encountered the liftman, a young man in his early thirties, who was always smiling. The lift was constantly busy, with people coming and going, yet every time I saw him, he had that same wide smile on his face. Curious, I asked him, "Don't you feel claustrophobic being in the lift for 10 hours a day?" He smiled even brighter and replied, "No sir, this is my home!" Despite the monotonous nature of his job, the liftman chose to focus on the positives. Instead of seeing the lift as a confined space, he viewed it as his home, a place where he could interact with people and spread positivity. Living life fully means finding joy in the small moments and embracing our circumstances with a positive attitude. It is about shifting our perspective to see the good in every situation.

Just ponder over this:

Human life is transient. Nobody will get out of this alive. A hundred years from now, none of us reading this today will be alive. Strangers will live in our homes. Eighty percent of everything that we are fighting so hard about will be immaterial. We will be remembered for a few years after we pass on, and then our history will slowly be put into oblivion. Similarly, if we go back another hundred years before us, none of those who fought, fretted, cheated, betrayed, killed are alive today, neither are the things relevant, which they did this for. It may sound funny to us now, but this is how we humans are, especially when it comes to money, power, greed or trying to be relevant.

If we focus on living our life to fullest, we could take the walks we have never taken, or sing the tune we never sang. If we could be genuinely happy for each other without any malice, jealousy, or comparison, we would live a worthy life that we could be proud of. In the end we all have to transit to the other side. It is just a question of who gets there first.

So, learn to appreciate the present moment, find contentment in everyday tasks, and always look for the silver lining. Life is a string of moments, but it happens only in this moment. If you live every moment in its entirety, you would have lived your life to its fullest.

Golden Rule:

Each moment offers a chance
to expand your horizons.
Find joy in the unexpected,
and live life to its fullest potential.

With Gratitude...

In their final moments, many people choose to leave behind a few last words – simple yet profound messages that reflect the essence of their lives. I've always been fascinated by these final expressions, often seeking them out to gain deeper wisdom about life. One story that particularly touched me was about a man who, in his last hours, shared this thought: "There is no such thing as time. Dying is like walking from the living room into the dining room. There are no beginnings and no endings." With these words, he took his final breath, passing away peacefully.

Curious to understand what others might say to their loved ones in their final moments, I conducted a small survey among close friends. I asked them to imagine themselves on their deathbeds, surrounded by loved ones, and to consider what wisdom they would want to impart as their last message. The response was overwhelming, and it formed the foundation of this book.

Here are some of the key insights that emerged,

Have Faith / Do Not Worry: Many would reassure their loved ones to trust in the process of life, embrace happiness, love themselves, and remain authentic.

Help Others / Give Back: A significant number would emphasise the importance of helping others, spreading love, expressing gratitude, forgiving, continuing to learn and grow, and living life to the fullest.

Mindfulness / Self-Reflection: Suggestions included meditating, responding instead of reacting, listening to oneself, following the heart, expressing oneself, and spending time with loved ones.

Personal Growth / Relationships: Some highlighted the importance of cultivating true relationships, travelling more, looking for signs, asking for help, taking care of health, and spending time with oneself.

I would like to express my heartfelt thanks to the following friends for their valuable contributions and encouragement, which played a crucial role in motivating me to write this book. Each name is important, and the order does not reflect their significance: Kshiti Pathak, Dr. Parul Bhatia, Puja Pushkarna, Rushi Shah, Sucheta Raval, Neetu Madan, Riddhima Mazumdar, Minal Parekh, Arvind Kiran, Nanak Varlani, Dr. Nikhil Zaveri, Dr. Jyotsna Prajapati, Hitesh Jeevan, Bichitra Mohapatra, Dr. Swati Makashir, Sanjay Pandita, Deepa Sriya Bhatnagar, Amarjeet Kaur Chhabra, Ruchika Mathur, Ashna Magon, Gauri Hajela, Parul Kumar, Dr. Varsha Sardana, SS Swani, Ramya Vengali, Neeta Samat, Rajendra Tuteja, Pranay Dugar, Saroj Prathypati, Shilpa Pagaria, Poonam Tandon, Dr. Sheela Raj, KS Ravikumar, Jayant Mehrotra, Jayaram Ramchandran, Rajesh Tandale, Indira Labde, Col. RN Singh, Sanjay Sharma, Shruti Segan Sharma, Dolon (Indrani) Acharya, Sneha Suvarna, Nikitaa Yash Soni, Asha Nair, Khyati Dharamsi, Chandra Balakrishnan, Ganga Sridhar, Punam Gupta, and Bakhtavar Mistry.

This book is a reflection of the wisdom shared by all of you, and I am deeply grateful for your input.

Santosh Joshi is a Life Coach, Past Life Regression Therapist, Trainer, Mentor, and Author of three bestsellers **KEYS – The secret to a happy and regret free life**, **Many Lives One Soul – Keys to deeper secrets**, and **SKY is Not the Limit**, and Founder of SKY Healing.

Santosh has spoken to thousands of people at conferences, colleges and companies as keynote speaker and growth catalyst, and through through his workshops. He is known for his deeper wisdom and insights conveyed through his unique style of story-telling. He has been able to reach out and help many people believe in themselves and live a fulfilling, successful, happy and regret free life.

Listen to Santosh Joshi by subscribing his Youtube channel

Wisdom Waves with Santosh

Follow Santosh Joshi online

santoshjoshi01

Connect with Santosh Joshi

+91 7506378779 info@santoshjoshi.com

OTHER BOOKS OF SANTOSH JOSHI